THE BELIEFNET GUIDE TO

# KABBALAH

THE BELIEFNET GUIDE TO

# KABBALAH

Arthur Goldwag

*Introduction by*
*Rabbi Lawrence Kushner*

Three Leaves Press

Doubleday / New York

PUBLISHED BY DOUBLEDAY
a division of Random House, Inc.

DOUBLEDAY is a registered trademark and Three Leaves Press and colophon
are trademarks of Random House, Inc.

All Bible quotes reprinted from *Tanakh*, © 1985, The Jewish Publication Society, with the
permission of the publisher, The Jewish Publication Society.

Excerpts from *Ehyeh: A Kabbalah for Tomorrow* © 2003 by Arthur Green (Woodstock, VT:
Jewish Lights Publishing). Permission granted by Jewish Lights Publishing, P.O. Box 237,
Woodstock, VT 05091, www.jewishlights.com.

Excerpt from *The Handbook of Jewish Meditation Practices: A Guide for Enriching the Sabbath
and Other Days of Your Life* © 2000 by David A. Cooper (Woodstock, VT: Jewish Lights
Publishing). Permission granted by Jewish Lights Publishing, P.O. Box 237, Woodstock, VT
05091, www.jewishlights.com.

Excerpts from *Tales of the Hasidim: The Early Masters/The Later Masters* by Martin Buber,
translated by Olga Marx, © 1947, 1948, copyright renewed 1975 by Schocken Books. Used
by permission of Schocken Books, a division of Random House, Inc.

Excerpts from *Major Trends in Jewish Mysticism* by Gershom Scholem, © 1946, 1954, and renewed 1974, 1982 by Schocken Books, a division of Random House, Inc.; Foreword © 1995
by Robert Alter. Used by permission of Schocken Books, a division of Random House, Inc.

Excerpts from *The Essential Kabbalah* © 1995 by Daniel C. Matt. Reprinted by permission
of HarperCollins Publishers, Inc.

Excerpts from vii, 59, 108–109, 215, 233–236 from *The Heart and the Fountain* by Joseph
Dan, © by Joseph Dan. Used by permission of Oxford University Press, Inc.

Library of Congress Cataloging-in-Publication Data

Goldwag, Arthur.
    The Beliefnet guide to Kabbalah / Arthur Goldwag ; introduction by
Lawrence Kushner.— 1st Three Leaves Press ed.
        p. cm.—(The Beliefnet guides ; 1)
    Includes bibliographical references.
    1. Cabala—History I. Title: Guide to the Kabbalah. II. Title. III. Series.
BM526.G56 2005
296.1'6—dc22                                    2004059892
ISBN 0-385-51453-0

PRINTED IN THE UNITED STATES OF AMERICA

June 2005

First Three Leaves Press Edition

10  9  8  7  6  5  4  3  2  1

# CONTENTS

*INTRODUCTION*

*BY RABBI LAWRENCE KUSHNER*  ix

*KABBALAH FAST FACTS*  xix


## 1. WHAT IS KABBALAH?

The Essence  6

A Brief History  9

Some Key Ideas  11

Non-Jewish Adaptations  14

Must Kabbalah Be Jewish to Be Authentic?  15


## 2. ORIGINS OF KABBALAH

The Roots of Kabbalah  19

Throne, Palace, and Creation: Three Early Schools of
Jewish Mysticism  22

*Bereshit* (Creation) Mysticism and the *Sefer Yezirah*  25

Early Kabbalah  31

## 3. THE RISE OF KABBALAH: THE *Zohar* AND RABBI ISAAC LURIA

From Provence to Gerona, Spain    43

The Ecstatic Kabbalah of Abraham Abulafia    45

The Problem of Evil: The "Left" Emanation    49

Ten Divine Emanations: The *Sefirot*    51

Characteristics of the *Sefirot*    54

The Four Worlds: Stages of Spiritual Ascent    63

The *Zohar:* The Heart of Kabbalah    67

Safed, Palestine, and Rabbi Isaac Luria ("The Ari")    71

The Lurianic Cosmology: *Tzimtzum, Shevirah,*
   and *Tikkun Olam*    75


## 4. A WOULD-BE MESSIAH, THE BAAL SHEM TOV, AND THE TWENTIETH CENTURY

The Myth of Joseph della Reina: Why the Messiah Still
   Hasn't Come    78

Hope and Catastrophe: The False Messiah Shabbetai Zevi    81

The Baal Shem Tov: A New Kind of Hasidism    87

The Twentieth Century: Jewish Mysticism Reborn    92


## 5. JEWISH MAGIC: AMULETS, DEMONS, AND THE USE OF NAMES


## 6. MEDITATIONS AT THE HEART OF KABBALAH

Imagine You Are Light—*Azriel of Gerona*    113

The Gates of Holiness—*Hayyim Vital*    113

A Meditation on the Tree of Life—*Tamar Frankiel*     115

A *Shema* Meditation     117

A Meditation on God's Name—*Arthur Green*     117

A Meditation on Raising Holy Sparks—*David Cooper*     118

## 7. A MINI-ANTHOLOGY OF KABBALAH

From *The Work of the Chariot*     122

From the *Zohar*     123

From Joseph Gikatilla's *Sha'arei Orah* (The Gates of Light)     129

From Moses Cordovero's *Or Ne'erav* (The Pleasant Light)     130

The Baal Shem Tov Opens the Gate     138

Martin Buber, from *Tales of the Hasidim*     141

## CONCLUSION: WHAT KABBALAH MEANS TO ME

### "A TOOL TO HELP ME GET AWAY FROM THE I, I, I"

AFTERWORD: GATHERING THE SPARKS BY RODGER KAMENETZ     154

GLOSSARY     158

NOTES     164

BIBLIOGRAPHY     167

Every generation has its own defining religious model—ethical monotheist, rationalist, humanist, social activist. For our time, the religious ideal seems to be moving toward the mystical. This shift began innocently enough as the desire for more intimately personal modes of organized religion or, as they have come to be known, spirituality. But, over the past few decades, this yearning for the spiritual has led increasing numbers of seekers to resurrect long-thought-dead mystical traditions and especially Judaism's own Kabbalah.

Suddenly, mystical is in. Signs of the first stirrings of a new paradigm abound: the appearance of the first volumes of the Pritzker-Matt translation of the *Zohar,* academic and popular conferences and seminars, rabbinic education, publishing houses, mainstream liturgies, adult education courses, celebrity testimonials, books like this one—all responding to a widespread, grassroots yearning. It is hard to imagine now but less than a generation ago mysticism was not even taught at rabbinic seminaries; there were virtually no popular books on Kabbalah, and, in Judaism, the word *mystic* was one of derision and scorn. Little wonder, then, that the topic still strikes us as strange and new. Charlatans, mountebanks, and charismatics abound.

That is why the book you are holding is so important and timely. In a lucid style and an easy-to-follow format, author Arthur Goldwag has succeeded in guiding us to the heart of the history and practice of Kabbalah. He offers us all a well-provisioned base camp as we commence our ascent toward ultimate knowing. It's no coincidence that Beliefnet.com, a website with a million members from many different faith traditions, has produced the present volume. It is a book for seekers. So let us begin our exploration of Jewish mysticism with some primary questions and definitions.

## WHO IS A MYSTIC?

A mystic is anyone who has the gnawing suspicion that the apparent discord, brokenness, contradictions, and discontinuities that assault us every day might conceal a hidden unity. Just beneath the apparent surface, everything is joined to everything else. To a mystic, therefore, what we call reality is but the myriad refractions of that ultimate, underlying unity. It is a Oneness in which all things—even and especially the self-consciousness of the mystic—are intermittently dissolved, annihilated. Now, only the One remains, or in Yiddish: *Alz ist Gott*—everything is God!

Such a definition obviously casts a wide net. It includes many people who probably don't usually consider themselves mystics—indeed, it deliberately includes anyone who might accidentally catch only a fleeting glimmer of the underlying unity. For only a moment, a bit of light sparkles through. This window might be laughing with a child, looking at a flower, or sitting at the bedside of a sick friend. In the words of the Hasidic maxim, nothing is beneath being a footstool for the holy. This certainly is not to deny that in every generation, there are those who are blessed with great mystical experiences and the poetic skill to be able to capture them in words. But, for the rest of us, encounters with the One are only momentary, and less dramatic. The roof does not fly off. The Mormon Tabernacle Choir does not sing. Light does not stream from our facial apertures. Such pyrotechnics are not a necessary precondition of being a mystic or for having a mystical experience. As long as the self is dissolved into the unity of all being, no matter how tame the effect, it is mystical. In other words, the book you are about to read might not just be about someone else; it might also be about you.

### WHERE IS GOD?

In order to better understand this melting or loss of self into the One, let us consider two models for understanding our relationship with God (or, if you prefer something less religious, then the Source of All Being).

The first model is classical, Western, vertical theism. It is the model with which most of us have been raised and which determines the syntax of most of our God-talk. God here can be represented by a big circle at the top and the individual by a tiny circle far below it. Obviously, in such a schema, God is *other* than creation. God is both vertically above and beyond it, presumably running it. He—and, since it's so inescapably hierarchical, God is naturally a "He"—may be actively and compassionately involved or dispassionately absent. God can be doing a good job of supervising creation or a lousy one. God gives us commandments, tells us to do things (don't murder, give charity, be nice), and we offer our own supplications and prayers—let me pass the exam, please make Johnny well again, stop war, and so forth. The key idea here is that God is outside, above and beyond the world; God is *other than* creation.

The second model initially has a more Eastern flavor, but we also find it in various forms throughout the history of religion in the West. According to this conception, God is still portrayed as a big circle. But the little circle representing the individual now lies *within* the big circle of God. Here God is literally all of being. God is simply all there is. *All reality is one and it is all God.* And therefore, the separateness, discreteness, "boundariedness," and autonomy of any one or any thing must be illusory. Everything is only a manifestation of God—and God obviously doesn't have any parts. God is the ocean and we are the waves. In the words of the prophet Isaiah, "The fullness of the whole earth is the presence of God!" (Isaiah 6:3)

This way of thinking turns many of the notions of a God who is above and other than creation on their head. Prayer is no longer a conversation. God can no longer be blamed for what goes wrong. God cannot intervene in the workings of the world. (Mystics, as you can now easily understand, are not much comfort as grief counselors.) In such a mystical model, prayer now becomes an occasion for contemplation of and meditation on our presence within the divine. Liturgy becomes a <u>mantra</u>. In such a model, what appears to be evil now only challenges us to try to comprehend how God could somehow be within it also. In such a system, you cannot have a relationship with a God of which you are already a dimension. You are simply made of it. You can contemplate how you are part of it but you cannot have a conversation with it. Ultimately, even the border between your consciousness and the divine becomes increasingly blurred. There is simply no God outside the system to whom you can complain, talk, or offer thanks. God is the One through whom everyone and everything is joined to everyone and everything. In the words of the old joke: What did the Zen monk say to the hot-dog vendor? Make me *one* with everything.

Since this experience of the mystic All is universal, every religion has its own mystical tradition, each with its own unique rituals and symbol sets. (Some scholars of religion go even as far as to maintain that mystical encounters are the touchstone for every organized religious tradition.) Beginning students of Judaism are often surprised to learn that it has several mystical traditions: the *Merkabah* or Chariot and *Heikhalot* or Heavenly Palace mysticism of second-century Palestine; Abulafian meditation in thirteenth-century Spain; the intricate Lurianic cosmology of sixteenth-century Safed; the Hasidic folk mysticism of eighteenth-century Eastern Europe; Abraham Isaac Kook's utopian mysticism in twentieth-century Israel; or, in the last generation, the extraordinary work of Martin Buber or Abraham Joshua Heschel. Nevertheless, when most people today speak of Jewish mysticism, they mean Kabbalah—a system that took shape in twelfth- and thirteenth-century Provence and

Castille, reaching its apogee with the appearance of the *Zohar* at the beginning of the fourteenth century. The kabbalistic mystical tradition in Judaism is so rich, well developed, influential, and widely known that, unless specified otherwise, Jewish mysticism and Kabbalah are, for all practical purposes, synonymous.

### WHAT IS KABBALAH?

What is Kabbalah?

The great Israeli scholar Moshe Idel once suggested that Kabbalah can be characterized by three unique ideas: *Ein Sof, Sefirot,* and *mitzvot,* to which I would add, Eros. God—that is, the Oneness in which all being is dissolved and from which being continuously emerges—is called, in Hebrew, *Ein Sof,* literally the One "without end." This is much more than simply the arithmetic concept of infinity. *Ein Sof* is neither numeric nor mathematical. It means, instead, without boundary, without definition, without any characteristics whatsoever. Indeed, to say anything about it at all violates the essential notion of the term. *Ein Sof* is the font, the source, the matrix, the substrate, the mother lode of being. It may also be being itself. It is to being what electricity is to the letters and words on a computer's video monitor. And, as anyone who has not conscientiously backed up his or her work knows, turn off the power and the letters and words are as if they had never been. For kabbalists, therefore, creation is not some event that happened in the past but a continuous and ever-present process. When we express

*a rich source or supply*

our gratitude for the world, it is because it has literally been created anew each day, each moment.

My youngest granddaughter, at age nine months, is just now beginning to make syllables. *Beh, beh, mah mah, da da.* Soon they will become the rubrics of words and sentences and ideas. With language she will begin to name and then learn how to intellectually manipulate her world. And, like the rest of us, she will doubtless begin to think that, since she has names for all the parts of reality, that reality indeed has all those parts. In this way, her world will become subdivided into myriad parts, each with its own name, geographic coordinates, descriptive characteristics, and, if it is human, with its own agenda. But then, hopefully, one day as a young woman, she will reencounter the Oneness of all being in which all words and all the parts of her world will be (re)dissolved. And the only word she will be able to use to describe it will be "Nothing"—that is, no thing, the One without beginning or end, *Ein Sof.*

A second characteristic of Kabbalah is the process through which this infinite One(ness) manifests itself and brings creation into being. Simply through being, by its very existence, there emerges from the One a series of concentric "emanations," or *Sefirot*—literally, in Hebrew, numbers. *Sefirot* are a metaphor for trying to comprehend how the One could possibly make this world of so many apparently discrete and discordant parts. The *Sefirot* themselves are alternatively described as dimensions of both the divine and of the human psyche and as the steps in the emanative process of creation, and, because everything is made of God, the *Sefirot* are also an image of the infrastructure of reality itself. Kabbalists are quick to caution, however, that even

xvi                    INTRODUCTION

though we speak of them as discrete entities, they are inseparable from the divine unity. Kabbalists see *Sefirot* everywhere; creation is a manifestation of the *Sefirot*. Every character, place,
even every color in the Hebrew Bible is an allusion to one of the
*Sefirot*. Indeed, the Bible itself can be read on a kabbalistic level
as a description of the interactive workings of the *Sefirot*. In the
same way, every dysfunction in our universe is likewise understood as the result of a destabilization of the *Sefirot*—which are
also the divine psyche. Performance of religious deeds now becomes a kind of repair of and maintenance for the divine. This
brings us to a third aspect of Kabbalah.

Classical Kabbalah is predicated on the idea that human beings, through acts of goodness, worship, love, healing, and
giving—or *mitzvot*—are able to influence the divine. In the
Aramaic maxim: *Al y'day itaruta dila-tata ba'ah itaruta d'l'ila*—
By means of awakening below comes awakening on High.
Kabbalah, in other words, necessarily involves the performance
of righteous deeds. The practitioner, as it were, becomes God's
chiropractor. We can easily understand therefore why Kabbalah
had such great appeal. It gave to the behavior of each individual Jew literally cosmic importance. Indeed, we suspect that
one litmus test of a would-be mystical experience is whether or
not it infuses its recipient with a heightened passion for righteous behavior.

Finally, to Idel's list, I would add Eros. While rabbinic Judaism had a well-developed notion of the *Shekhinah* as the
feminine, in-dwelling presence of God, Kabbalah developed an
elaborate and often sexually explicit theology of sexuality. God
now had male and female sides, a Hebrew yin–yang in which

*powder*
*which*
*turns*
*blue or*
*red*
*depending*
*on its*
*alkalinity*
*(blue) or*
*acidity (red)*

the feminine became an equal partner—all portrayed through Sefirotic allusion and imagery. Erotic love becomes, if not a sacrament, then a religious act affecting worlds far beyond the two earthly lovers themselves. Righteousness restores a balance and harmony to the male and female dimensions of a One that has no dimensions. _warning or caution_

One final caveat. Not everything called mysticism, of course, is mysticism. Because Kabbalah claims to offer knowledge of the inner workings of creation, we can understand how superstition and magic came to be associated with it in popular folk culture. Indeed, even today we carelessly assume that if something is otherworldly, paranormal, mysterious, awesome, magical, or just plain creepy, it is mystical. This includes ghosts, dybbuks, golems, weird dreams, bizarre coincidences, Bible codes, and secret incantations, as well as mostly everything in the general category of "Beam me up, Scotty." Anything claiming knowledge of how to manipulate ultimate reality becomes mystical. It was doubtless such associations with superstition that led nineteenth- and early-twentieth-century rationalists to reject anything mystical and throw the baby out with the bathwater. Indeed, for most of the past century, references to the Jewish mystical tradition were effectively purged from the history books. We feel like amnesiacs.

In the conclusion of this book, Arthur Goldwag interviews a rabbinical student who discovered Kabbalah after a long journey through the New Age and political activism. "Enlightenment," he says, "isn't something where one day you're not and then one day you are and that's that. It's about glimpses. Mystical awareness is a time when there are no words, when thought ceases, when the constant stream of thought, the gap between one thought and the other, expands. That's the aim: to expand those moments. It doesn't have to be Jewish, and it doesn't have to be intellectual—any practice you do for a long time will help you get there."

So, let us begin, again.

# KABBALAH FAST FACTS
*From Beliefnet*

Kabbalah is a mystical way of interpreting the Torah, the primary Jewish scriptures, and of attempting to understand God. Practitioners believe the study of Kabbalah can help unlock the secrets of the universe.

Kabbalah literally means "that which is received." The teachings of Kabbalah, at first never written down, were supposed to be passed directly by word of mouth from teacher to student.

In Kabbalah, God is called *Ein Sof.* In Hebrew, *Ein Sof* means "without end." The name symbolizes God's lack of boundaries in time and space.

*Ein Sof* interacts with the world through ten manifestations, or emanations, known as the ten *Sefirot.* The ten *Sefirot* are as follows:

- *Keter*–Crown
- *Hochma*–Wisdom
- *Binah*–Understanding
- *Hesed*–Kindness
- *Gevurah*–Strength
- *Tif'eret*–Beauty
- *Netzah*–Victory
- *Hod*–Awe
- *Yesod*–Foundation
- *Shekhinah* or *Malkhut*–Presence

The ten *Sefirot* are often represented by a diagram referred to as the Kabbalah tree of life.

Tradition teaches that one must reach the age of forty before beginning to explore Kabbalah. Younger people are not considered to have the necessary background or emotional maturity to be able to deal with the topic.

Kabbalists believe that the mystical system was revealed by God at the same time as the revelation of the Torah, and that each letter in the Torah has an underlying, secret significance.

The *Zohar,* a mystical commentary on the Torah, is the primary Kabbalah text. It is usually traced to thirteenth-century Spain. Most scholars believe it was written by Spanish kabbalist Moses de Leon, though some claim it was penned by the second-century sage Rabbi Shimon bar Yochai.

The golden age of Jewish mysticism occurred in the sixteenth century in Safed, a city in northern Israel, when Jews expelled from Spain during the Inquisition gathered there. Great kabbalists and scholars during this time included Rabbi Joseph Caro, Rabbi Moses Cordovero, and Rabbi Solomon Alkabez.

Rabbi Isaac Luria is often regarded as the greatest kabbalist. He is known by the acronym for his Hebrew name, ha-Ari, "the Lion."

In the eighteenth century, the Baal Shem Tov used kabbalistic teachings as the basis for the formation of his new sect, Hasidism.

The modern study and scholarship of Kabbalah was spearheaded by the work of German-born Gershom Scholem, who lived from 1897 to 1982.

# 1

# What Is Kabbalah?

*Be prepared for thy God, oh Israelite! Make thyself ready to direct thy heart to God alone. Cleanse the body and choose a lonely house where none shall hear thy voice. Sit there in thy closet and do not reveal thy secret to any man. . . . Cleanse thy clothes, and, if possible, let all thy garments be white, for all this is helpful in leading the heart toward the fear of God and the love of God.*

—RABBI ABRAHAM ABULAFIA (CA. 1240–1291)

The very word *Kabbalah* implies something sinister and furtive. Cabals (see page 2) hatch conspiracies behind closed doors; cabbalistic matters are by definition dark and obscure. But what exactly is Kabbalah? If you have a smattering of religious literacy, you know that it has something to do with Judaism (though it is not a denomination or movement, like Reform, Conservative, Orthodox, or Reconstructionist). If you've spent any time browsing the shelves in the New Age section of your local bookstore, you'll know that it pertains to magical beliefs and practices, everything from palmistry, numerology, astrology, time travel, and reincarnation to summoning demons and raising the dead, but mostly to mysticism—the felt conviction that there is a sacred, underlying unity to the world and that the divine presence can be experienced directly, rather than through the intermediary of organized religion. To that end, Kabbalah involves meditation, ecstatic dance, chanting, and other practices that are reminiscent of Sufism (the mystical form of Islam) and many Eastern religions.

---
How Come?
---

### Are Cabals Kabbalistic?

Some people claim that the word *cabal* (meaning a small group of secret plotters) originated in Restoration England as an acronym for Charles II's hated inner circle of advisors: Clifford of Chudleigh, Ashley (Lord Shaftesbury), Buckingham (George Villiers), Arlington (Henry Bennet), and Lauderdale (John Maitland). Indeed, this group was referred to by that name, but the word had already acquired its meaning. It entered the English language in the early sixteen hundreds by way of the French, who took it from *cabala,* the Latin spelling of the Hebrew word Kabbalah, which means "tradition" or "receiving."

---

Type the word *Kabbalah* into an Internet search engine and you'll be directed to hundreds of websites expounding halakhic (meaning it's in strict conformity with biblical law), *Chassidut* (meaning it's in conformity with Hasidic beliefs and practices), feminist, and modern Kabbalah, speculative and practical Kabbalah, Christian and Gnostic Cabala, and Hermetic Qabala, to name only a few of the available varieties and spellings. Bearded, black-hatted rebbes teach "kosher Kabbalah" as an essential facet of strictly Orthodox Jewish observance; other teachers—Jewish and non-Jewish alike—explore Kabbalah in the context of Buddhism, Tantric meditation, political activism, and even ecology. Practitioners of Qaballah are as likely as not to be pagans or Wiccans. Kabbalah Centres all over the world teach Kabbalah as a "spiritual technology" that "creates order out of chaos," while healing the body and soul. The "New Kabbalah" endeavors to integrate the teachings of the medieval Jewish sage Isaac Luria (1534–1572) with modern secular thinkers like Freud and Derrida; a tiny organization in California is attempting to revive Shabbetainism, the seventeenth-century movement that believed that a kabbalistic rabbi named Shabbetai Zevi (1626–1676) was the Messiah.

Kabbalah looms large in high and low secular culture. It figures in literary classics like Mary Shelley's *Frankenstein* (which was probably inspired by a Jacob Grimm story about a Kabbalistic sorcerer) and the visionary poems of William Blake (who would have learned about it through its Christian permutations, particularly in the writings of the Swedish mystic Emanuel Swedenborg), and in popular contemporary novels like Myla Goldberg's *Bee Season*. In 1997 a bestseller, *The Bible Code*, purported to use state-of-the-art computer technology wedded to kabbalistically inspired algorithms (see page 4) to derive terrifying apocalyptic prophecies from the Bible. A few years ago Leonard Nimoy, *Star Trek*'s Mr. Spock, created a small scandal when he published a book called *Shekhinah* (after the Hebrew appellation for the divine presence), which featured his gauzy photographs of scantily clad female models wrapped in *tefillin* (leather boxes containing quotations from the Bible that Orthodox Jews strap to their arms and head for morning prayers) and talliths (prayer shawls). And of course there's Madonna, whose embrace of Kabbalah has drawn so much controversy and who

--- How Come? ---

### Mystical Numerology

The characters used for Hebrew letters are also used to represent numbers. When biblical words and passages are read as numbers instead of words, another level of meaning can be revealed. This has inspired an entire school of biblical exegesis known as *Gematria*. This practice long predates Kabbalah—its origins, in fact, are not even Jewish. The first recorded number–letter substitution was an eighth-century B.C.E. inscription of the Babylonian king Sargon II, which declared that a wall had been built a certain length to correspond with the numerical value of his name. One of the most famous *Gematria* can be found in the Christian Bible, in Revelation: When "Nero Caesar" is written in its seven Hebrew consonants, they yield a value of 50 + 200 + 6 + 50 + 100 + 60 + 200, which adds up to 666, the so-called "Number of the Beast." The medieval German Kabbalists *(Hasidei Ashkenaz)* made great use of *Gematria,* in prayers and meditations, in commentaries on laws—and for making amulets and performing magic.

Many Jews regard *Gematria* with discomfort as something more ingenious than profound—if the numerical codes are elaborate enough (à la *The Bible Code)* the interpreter can derive almost any meaning at all from a given Hebrew text. In general, numerology plays a much more central role in Christian and Hermetic versions of Kabbalah.

has adopted a Jewish name, "Esther." The former Material Girl uses kabbalistic symbols in her videos, has written a series of children's books based on kabbalistic themes, and sends her daughter to a Kabbalah after-school program. We've all seen those ubiqui-

———————————————— How Come? ————————————————

*What's with the Red String?*

Stars like Demi Moore, Winona Ryder, Madonna—and even Madonna's daughter Lourdes—wear a braided "Kabbalah bracelet" made out of red string to protect them from the evil eye—"the unfriendly stare and unkind glances we sometimes get from people around us," as the Kabbalah Centre, which sells the string for twenty-six dollars a length, defines it.

The evil eye is a common superstition throughout the Mediterranean region. It is believed to be a sort of curse that is transmitted, often inadvertently or unconsciously, when someone looks at you or your possessions (or especially your children) with envy. The Italians call it *mal occhio,* the Spanish *mal ojo.* It is *jettatore* in Sicilian, and *bla band* in Farsi. In Yiddish the red string is called a *roite bendel.* One nonsupernatural explanation of its efficacy is that it reminds its wearer to bear himself or herself with humility, so as not to attract envy.

There are biblical traditions associated with the red string as well. In Genesis, when Tamar was in labor with her twins Pharez and Zarah, the midwife tied a red string around Zarah's wrist to identify him as the firstborn. A red string was tied around the horn of the scapegoat on Yom Kippur; after the animal was killed, tradition tells us, the thread would miraculously turn white.

And there is an ancient tradition of wrapping a red string around the matriarch Rachel's tomb seven times. Properly blessed, this string is supposed to have powers to protect pregnant women and, indeed, to ward off the evil eye. In the *Zohar,* Rachel's tomb is explicitly associated with the *Shekhinah,* the Kabbalistic term for the divine presence.

tous red string bracelets (page 5) sold by the Kabbalah Centre, jewelry stores, and other purveyors of fine religious and fashion accessories—and worn by Madonna, Paris Hilton, Demi Moore, and Britney Spears in photographs.

### THE ESSENCE

Which of these Kabbalahs is authentic? Although there are important kabbalistic texts, there has never been one canonical "Book of Kabbalah," nor are there synagogues or temples that practice it exclusively (though Kabbalah plays a large role in all Hasidic sects). There is no formula of faith, no credo that boils it down to a well-turned phrase.

So what *is* Kabbalah? It is not simply Jewish mysticism. There have been many Jewish mystics who were not kabbalists; there have even been a few kabbalists who weren't mystics. The literal meaning of the Hebrew word *kabbalah* is "tradition" or "receiving." The name suggests doctrines that were received by revelation in the ancient past and handed down through the generations; also that its teachers transmitted it one-on-one to select students. Joseph Dan, the Gershom Scholem Professor of Kabbalah at Hebrew University in Jerusalem, offers a fairly precise definition: "The Kabbalah is a Jewish esoterical tradition of contemplation of divine secrets, believed to have been given by God to Moses on Mt. Sinai, which includes spiritual expressions of a variety of disciplines and characteristics."

Kabbalists believe that if we learn how to open ourselves up, to think beyond the surfaces of things, if we master meditative techniques that allow us to break out of the daily world, we can experience the presence of God. By far the most important Kabbalistic practice, just as in traditional Judaism, is study of the Torah (the first five books of the Bible, attributed to Moses). Kabbalists believe that Moses' revelation at Mt. Sinai—the greatest of all "receivings"—is still going on today. Kabbalah teaches us how to read the Torah in the deepest possible ways—literally, to decode it. In the words of the great scholar Gershom Scholem (1897–1982), who did more than anyone to bring the Jewish Kabbalah to the attention of the secular world:

> [The Torah] does not consist merely of chapters, phrases, and words; rather is it to be regarded as the living incarnation of the divine wisdom which eternally sends out new rays of light. It is not merely the historical law of the Chosen People, although it is that too; it is rather the cosmic law of the Universe, as God's wisdom conceived it. Each configuration of letters in it, whether it makes sense in human speech or not, symbolizes some aspect of God's creative power which is active in the universe.

Kabbalists not only believe that we can commune with God; they believe they can tap into His divine powers. This is heady stuff. Misunderstood or applied inappropriately, this notion can also be quite dangerous. Whether or not you believe in the supernatural, the ideas behind Kabbalah can lead the unwary or the impulsive to heresy, grandiosity or insanity; if you do believe in the supernatural, then it's self-evident that the powers Kabbalah unlocks are potentially deadly. For centuries kabbalists, no matter how much they disagreed among themselves about other matters, were united in the belief that their ideas were not for general consumption (see below). Only stable, mature, educated men of unimpeachable faith and character were

──────────── How Come? ────────────

*Kabbalah Is Not for Everyone*

According to Rabbi Dennis Gura of the Kehillat Ma'arav, the Westside Congregation in Santa Monica, California: "G-d intoxication is dangerous. . . . The divine can, must be scary, frightening, dangerous." A parable in the Babylonian Talmud *(Hagigah* 14b) is frequently cited as a cautionary tale about the dangers of mystical speculation: Four rabbis, Simeon ben Azzai, Ben Zoma, Elisha ben Avuya, and Rabbi Akiva, entered *pardes* or paradise (also translated as "the garden" or "the orchard"). According to the tale, Ben Azzai looked and died. Ben Zoma looked and was driven insane. Avuya "cut the shoots" (meaning that he despoiled the garden—the historical Elisha ben Avuya adopted the heresy of Gnostic dualism and abandoned rabbinic Judaism). Only Rabbi Akiva entered in peace and left in peace.

The interpretation: The four rabbis were meditating; the garden they entered was psychic rather than physical. Nonetheless, the dangers were real. Only the great Rabbi Akiva, a towering figure in rabbinic Judaism (born in 50 C.E. and martyred by the Romans in 135 C.E., Rabbi Akiva is regarded as perhaps the greatest Talmudic scholar who ever lived), was learned, mature, and stable enough to survive unscathed the direct encounter with the divine presence. Interestingly enough, Akiva, who started out in life as an illiterate shepherd, didn't even begin to study Torah until he was forty.

permitted to learn Kabbalah's secrets—some teachers required their students to be married men of at least forty years of age (age twenty was sufficient for others, provided the young aspirants had attained a sufficient level of learning). But that still doesn't answer the question: What is Kabbalah?

## A BRIEF HISTORY

Narrowly defined, Kabbalah is a Jewish tradition that flowered in Provence and the Rhine Valley in the eleven hundreds, with roots extending as far away as Palestine and Babylonia and at least as deep in time as the second century C.E. Kabbalah sought to explain how the universe was created (and how it will end), how God is manifested in creation, and most important, how to experience the divine presence for oneself. By the twelve hundreds, the vital center of kabbalism had moved to Spain, where the great book the *Zohar* was "discovered." After Ferdinand and Isabella expelled the Jews in the 1490s, Palestine became the locus of kabbalism, especially the town of Safed in the Galilee, where the great Rabbi Isaac Luria taught.

By the seventeenth century, Kabbalah was so influential it had virtually become the standard Jewish theology. But in the second half of that century it suffered a major setback when a brilliant twenty-year-old kabbalistic rabbi known as Nathan of Gaza (1643–1680) prophesied the sultan of Turkey's imminent surrender of his throne to the Messiah, whom he had identified as an emotionally unstable, Smyrna-born rabbi named Shabbetai Zevi. When the sultan offered this would-be Messiah a choice between execution or conversion to Islam, Zevi chose the latter, devastating and disappointing those adherents who didn't follow him into apostasy.

The fallout from the Shabbetain heresy, as it was called, was shattering, but Kabbalah continued on, thanks to Hasidism, which began as a mass movement in Germany and Eastern Europe in the seventeen hundreds. Though once considered revolutionary, the Hasidim, with their Old World black outfits and separatist traditions, are now thought of as the most traditional of traditional Jews.

As the Enlightenment took hold in the eighteenth century, most of organized Judaism began to distance itself from the more exotic manifestations of mysticism. Reform Judaism was born and took on many of the trappings of Protestantism, frowning on the superstitions and excesses of Kabbalah. Jews who were gifted at numbers occupied themselves with physics and mathematics instead of *Gematria* (finding meanings in the numeric qualities of Hebrew words in the Bible—see page 4); the visionary passages of the Bible and Talmud were interpreted as parables and metaphors for ethical and moral teachings and the yearning for the literal Messiah was transformed into secular Zionism and a generalized sense of social responsibility. Not until the advent of the Jewish Renewal movement in America in the 1960s (a movement that melds communalism, feminism, political radicalism, and Jewish mysticism) did Kabbalah begin to reassert itself as a force within the mainstream of Judaism.

### SOME KEY IDEAS

The key ideas of Kabbalah follow from its novel cosmogony, or story of creation. Kabbalists believed that the letters of the Hebrew alphabet comprise the building blocks of the universe and that God—whose Essence is indescribable—can nevertheless be apprehended in the form of ten separate but interconnected emanations called the *Sefirot*.

The most influential teacher of Kabbalah was undoubtedly Rabbi Luria. According to Luria, things went terribly awry at the moment of creation. The world we live in, he said, is made of the fragments of the universe that God had intended to create, but which literally burst while He was assembling it. Some of these shards still carry traces of the divine light. So long as they are polluted by matter, those sparks are the source of evil. If the world is ever to be redeemed, human intervention is required.

In Luria's teachings, the Jewish ethical obligation to purify one's self and "repair the world" (known as *tikkun olam*) was taken literally. Every good deed that a Jew committed, every mandated prayer and ritual obligation that he or she performed, each of the 613 Torah commandments fulfilled, freed one of those stray sparks from the gross, corrupting matter it was trapped in and returned it to God, purging a little bit of evil from the world and bringing it that much closer to what God had intended it to be. In the Kabbalah of Luria, prayer and observance were not just passive gestures of piety and obedience; they were part of the divine work of creation—they had the power to change the universe. When the work of repair was completed, the Messiah would arrive, bringing a new world into being.

These may be the most salient intellectual components of Kabbalah, but they hardly exhaust it, nor do they make up a coherent philosophical system. Though Kabbalah grapples with the most profound moral and philosophical questions—cosmology and eschatology (the beginning and the end of the world), the origins of evil, and the nature of time and space—its expositors were visionaries rather than formal thinkers: their writings are mythological and symbolical rather than rational. To these mystics, God wasn't an Aristotelian or deistic abstraction, the requisite "prime mover" who set the clockwork of creation into motion before departing to attend to His own business, nor was He an incorporeal, almighty king who promulgated laws and meted out rewards and punishments (though He was that too)—He was a palpable, all-pervasive presence: not just the source of all things but their essence. Nor was He a "He"—if God's immanence, the *Shekhinah* (the divine presence that you relate to when you're in the midst of heartfelt prayer or experiencing a mystical rapture), was often described as feminine (indeed, it was frequently eroticized as such), the Deity transcended gender or any other descriptive attribution.

But if God defies direct description, kabbalistic adepts nonetheless communed with Him and believed that they channeled His divine powers. In the mid–twelve hundreds, Rabbi Abraham Abulafia, very likely influenced by the Sufis (mystically inclined adherents of Islam), devised complex meditations that, if they were followed to the letter, would induce ecstatic experiences that led to prophecy. *Tzaddik*s (literally, righteous ones) were said to perform wonders—seemingly miraculous

works of magic and healing. Kabbalists studied and practiced
magic and astrology; they expounded complex demonologies
and angelologies; they posited multiple worlds and parallel
universes. They knew how to ward off—and how to deliver—
deadly curses. Some of them, legend has it, could even create
life (see page 29).

As if the ideas of Kabbalah weren't sufficiently challenging
and contradictory, many kabbalistic texts are virtually impossible to understand. Many of these teachings passed through
multiple translations and traveled great distances, often under
terrible conditions (the destruction of the Second Temple, the
persecution of the Jews during the Crusades and the Spanish
Inquisition, and the pogroms of the Cossacks all coincide with
great epochs in the history of Kabbalah), before they were set
into print. Some kabbalistic writings were transcripts of dreams
and visions. And some of them are incomprehensible *by design*.
Esoteric in the strictest definition of the term, the Kabbalah was
explicitly intended for the few. Some of its most important rev-
elations are only alluded to with tantalizing hints. It's possible
that kabbalists deliberately allowed corrupt or incomplete versions of important texts to be published, as a way of baffling the
uninitiated.

More often, key texts weren't published at all. Rabbi Hayyim
Vital (1542–1620), Rabbi Luria's leading disciple, refused to allow any of his books to be published during his lifetime. Gershom Scholem has described a treatise he wrote called "The
Gates of Holiness," a comprehensive guide to the mystical way
of life. Its fourth chapter summarized centuries of kabbalistic
teachings on practical techniques to induce prophecy. But when

the book finally found its way into print, that chapter was replaced by the following statement: "Thus speaks the printer:
This fourth part will not be printed, for it is all holy names and
secret mysteries which it would be unseemly to publish."


### NON-JEWISH ADAPTATIONS

As early as the fourteen hundreds there were attempts to syn-
thesize Christian and Jewish esoteric learning with the objective of bringing more converts into the Christian fold. Thus, the
so-called Christian Cabala and Hermetic Qabala got their start.
The young Platonic philosopher Giovanni Pico della Miran-
dola (1463–1494) inspired great excitement (and controversy)
throughout the learned Christian world when he commis-
sioned Latin translations of various kabbalistic texts, offering
them as proof of his claim that "no science can better convince
us of the divinity of Jesus Christ than magic and the Kabbalah."
After Cornelius Agrippa of Nettesheim (1486–1535) completed his encyclopedic *De Occulta Philosophia* in 1531, Kabbalah became inextricably associated with witchcraft and the
occult. The writings of many alchemists of the sixteenth century frequently alluded to Kabbalah; and in the seventeen hundreds kabbalistic symbols, such as pillars and certain Hebrew
letters, were adopted by the Freemasons. Rosicrucianism, a synthesis of ancient Egyptian religion, Neoplatonism, Gnosticism,
and a veritable stew of other arcane influences, contributed to
the Hermetic Qabala, which was at the heart of the theory and
practice of the Hermetic Order of the Golden Dawn, the

hugely influential nineteenth-century British occult society, and its many successors in the present-day New Age movement.

But is any of this really Kabbalah?

## MUST KABBALAH BE JEWISH TO BE AUTHENTIC?

The original Kabbalists never had any doubt that what they were doing was intrinsically Jewish. Students of the Kabbalah by definition were deeply versed in the Torah and Talmud and halakhically committed (this means they strived to obey all of the commandments in the Torah). "Even after one has achieved the spirituality of an angel, one must still abide by the commandments like a simple Jew," declared the Baal Shem Tov (1698–1760), the founder of modern Hasidism.

Nowadays the teachers at a Kabbalah Centre might tell you that you don't have to be observant or even Jewish, that you don't have to know Torah, indeed, that you needn't learn Hebrew or Aramaic to benefit from studying the *Zohar* in its original language. Merely looking at ("scanning") the shapes of the letters will provide profound benefits, they say, because "Hebrew letters are the DNA of the soul, scanning helps to reprogram our soul for greater positivity." (Imbibing a bottle of "Kabbalah water," available at Kabbalah Centre stores for approximately twelve dollars per gallon, promotes "healing, well-being, and rejuvenation" as well.)

Is Kabbalah only authentic when it's propounded by and for Jews? What if you are Jewish but not deeply religious? Perhaps you feel more comfortable meditating on a name of God than a mantra assigned by a TM instructor. Maybe you're intrigued by the notion of the *Shekhinah*, which is sometimes imagined as a Jewish "goddess." Are you permitted to pick and choose from Kabbalah's spiritual repertory? Or is it an all-or-nothing proposition? Does anyone have an exclusive claim on Kabbalah?

Kabbalah may be ancient but it is not a relic, something that exists in a pure, unadulterated state. Gershom Scholem's extensive writings have shown how Zoroastrianism, Neoplatonism, Sufism, Christian Gnosticism, and varieties of Christian mysticism all exerted an influence on its development, and Kabbalah has never stopped evolving. Even the most observant, tradition-bound Hasidim teach a different Kabbalah today than their parents and grandparents did. The egalitarian, multicultural, and politically progressive mysticism that the Jewish Renewal leader Rabbi Zalman Schachter-Shalomi espouses (in settings and to congregations that can look more like Grateful Dead concerts than worship services) would be unrecognizable (and in many ways abhorrent) to his teachers at the Lubavitcher Yeshiva in Brooklyn, where he was ordained in 1947.

Mystics, no matter what their religious affiliation—Christian, Buddhist, Hindu, and Muslim alike—all aspire to the same experiences. Kabbalah can be a legitimate object of fascination and inspiration for nonobservant Jews, and even for non-Jews. How could it be otherwise, when Judaism itself is so heterogeneous—and when so much of mainstream Judaism disdains and rejects mysticism? Surely an open-minded seeker from a different faith (or no established faith at all) is more likely to appreciate the poetry of the *Zohar* than a Jew who is wholly committed to secular humanism. "God isn't only for Jews," writes the scholar Tamar Frankiel. "So neither is Kabbalah."

But with one important reservation. Whereas mystic traditions do indeed share similar aspirations, they cannot be understood apart from their particular religious contexts. "There is no such thing as mysticism in the abstract," Gershom Scholem famously declared in his *Major Trends in Jewish Mysticism*. Kabbalah emerged from rabbinic Judaism. Even the least esoteric aspects of Kabbalah assume a deep familiarity with the *Tanakh* (the Hebrew Bible) and the Talmud, in their original Hebrew and Aramaic. If you don't have to be Jewish to learn from Kabbalah, neither should you lose sight of the fact that Kabbalah is Jewish through and through. It can no more be separated from Judaism than the mysticism of St. John of the Cross can be viewed apart from Catholicism, or the poetry of Rumi divorced from Islam.

Any approach to Kabbalah that treats it primarily as a magical tool kit, a self-help program, or a spiritual cure-all is intrinsically suspect. On the other hand, you needn't be put off by dogmatic Jews who insist that the Kabbalah belongs to them alone. As the contemporary mystic scholar Arthur Green writes in *Ehyeh*, his superb introduction to Kabbalah, Kabbalah teaches that

> God and world are deep structure and surface of the same
> reality. This means that knowing God, knowing the
> world, and authentic self-knowledge are all aspects of the
> same search for truth. The same is true on the plane of
> emotion: love of God, love of all creatures, and proper
> self-love cannot be separated from one another. To wor-

ship God is to live with reverence, to treat all beings, including oneself (this is often the hardest part!) as embodiments of the single Being.

If all creation aspires to unity, then by what right can any creature presume to exclude his or her fellow creatures from exploring a spiritual path? So long as they're respectful; so long as they don't seek to appropriate it for their own nonspiritual purposes; so long as they don't deny or disparage or distort or insult its essential Jewishness (even if they don't subscribe to it themselves), all are invited to partake in the wisdom of Kabbalah.

The following chapters are written for anyone, Jewish or non-Jewish, observant or nonobservant, who is interested in learning more about this indescribably rich and fascinating Jewish mystical tradition. Though a little book like this can hardly attempt to do more than scratch the surface of a subject as vast and challenging as Kabbalah, I hope it will strike a few small sparks, and perhaps even open up a few hearts and minds.

# 2

# ORIGINS OF KABBALAH

*Above the expanse over their heads was the semblance of a throne, in ap-*
*pearance like sapphire; and on top, upon this semblance of a throne, there*
*was the semblance of a human form. From what appeared as his loins up,*
*I saw a gleam as of amber—what looked like a fire encased in a frame; and*
*from what appeared as his loins down, I saw what looked like fire. There*
*was a radiance all about him. Like the appearance of the bow which shines*
*in the clouds on a day of rain, such was the appearance of the surrounding*
*radiance. That was the appearance of the semblance of the Presence of the*
*Lord.*

—EZEKIEL 1:26

## THE ROOTS OF KABBALAH

Some ultra-traditional Jews still insist that Kabbalah begins
with Abraham—that the biblical patriarch not only personally
authored the *Sefer Yezirah*, Kabbalah's oldest text, but used the
supernatural powers it teaches to convince his neighbors that
they should follow the one God. But most scholars today date
the first great flowering of Jewish mysticism to within a few
generations after the fall of the Second Temple, in the second
century C.E. This coincides with the beginnings of rabbinic Judaism and the composition of the Talmud, or Oral Torah.

But Jewish mysticism itself doesn't begin there; its roots go back to the Bible itself. The patriarchs and Moses and the prophets, most notably Ezekiel, some seven hundred years before the rabbinic era, had all spoken with God. Ezekiel's account of the celestial chariot pulled by winged creatures and topped by "the semblance of a throne," upon which sat "the appearance of the semblance of the Presence of the Lord" (excerpted above), was considered the most detailed and convincing revelation of celestial matters in the Bible. In the centuries before the fall of the Second Temple and the rise of Christianity, ascetic and apocalyptic sects like the Essenes, pious Jews like Jesus of Nazareth, and the authors of pseudepigrapha (ancient texts with biblical themes and characters that were not included in the biblical canon) like those found in the Dead Sea Scrolls—*The Book of Enoch*, for example—had cultivated mystical experiences through intensive prayer, solitude, fasting, and guided meditations.

Jewish mysticism didn't form in a vacuum. Pythagoreanism, a Hellenic form of mysticism, with its mystical numerology and ideas about the transmigration of souls (both of which would reemerge in Kabbalah), had been circulating throughout the Middle East since the fifth century B.C.E.; the Persian religion known as Zoroastrianism was highly influential as well. As early as the first century C.E. Gnosticism had attracted many—Christian and Jewish alike—into adopting heretical notions like dualism (the belief that God's power is not absolute, and that the world we live in is the creation of a separate deity, a demiurge, who is the source of evil). Starting in the third century C.E., many of the ideas and the specific vocabulary of Neoplatonism would be incorporated into Jewish mysticism. (Devised by the philosopher Plotinus [204–270 c.e.] Neoplatonism proposed that all matter devolves from a transcendent "Godhead" in progressively "thickening" stages, like water cascading from a fountain, and that through contemplation it is possible to lift one's spirit back to the highest level and reunite with it.) With their descriptions of divine emanations and their enumerations of demons and angels—including potentates like Metatron (see below), who is sometimes described as a virtual surrogate for God (one of his many names is

### Who Is Metatron?

Metatron is an immensely powerful angel who also goes by seventy-two other names. According to the apocryphal *Book of Enoch,* Enoch (the father of Methuselah, and Noah's great-grandfather) didn't die; instead, God transformed him into Metatron. In some texts he is described as a heavenly scribe; some say he is the angel in Genesis who stopped Abraham from sacrificing his son Isaac and wrestled with Jacob. In other texts he acts as a surrogate deity, enjoying full responsibility for all earthly affairs. Metatron was important to the founder of the Mormons, Joseph Smith, because of Enoch's association with the celestial city of Zion. In our own day, the rock guitarist Carlos Santana credits Metatron with his renewed popularity. In an interview with *Rolling Stone* magazine, he revealed that Metatron visited him while he was meditating one day to deliver the following message: "You will be inside the radio frequency for the purpose of connecting the molecules with the light." Sure enough, Santana's next recording, *Superstition,* was a multiplatinum hit.

"The Lesser Yahweh")—even the earliest texts of Jewish mysticism tested the boundaries of monotheism and conventional Judaism.

Rabbinic tradition had long regarded piety, punctilious observance, and profound Torah study as sufficient in themselves to bring one into the presence of God (what has been called a "moderate mysticism"), but it also quietly accommodated an ecstatic, intensive strain of mysticism as well. The Talmud itself discloses that some of its greatest scholars, sages like Rabbi Akiva, not only parsed biblical texts and argued the fine points of the law, but meditated, chanted, and utilized other yogi-like practices to imbue themselves with the prophetic spirit. Some of them practiced magic as well.

### THRONE, PALACE, AND CREATION:
### THREE EARLY SCHOOLS OF JEWISH MYSTICISM

Three major schools of specifically Jewish mystic literature date from the rabbinic era: *Merkabah* (chariot or throne), *Heikhalot* (palace or chambers), and *Bereshit* (creation, literally "in the beginning"). All of them would have an important influence on the Kabbalah, when it emerged in the next millennium.

Meditating on the prophet Ezekiel's vision of the heavenly throne and chanting ecstatically, *Merkabah* mystics ascended out of the world to behold the flaming chariot and its attendant cherubim for themselves. *Heikhalot* mystics not only attained the precincts of heaven but explored its labyrinthine chambers and palaces, braving rivers of fire, passing through multiplicities of firmaments, and meeting challenges from hierarchically ordered hosts of angelic sentries who inspected the amulets that they carried and demanded that they recite secret passwords (usually secret names of God) before granting them safe passage, instantly putting to death those unfortunates who failed the test.

Those who survived to tell the tale brought back eyewitness reports of fantastic worlds and detailed accounts of conversations with powerful supernatural beings (transcribers were frequently stationed next to the entranced adepts to take down their visions as they occurred). Many of them saw God Himself and were able to take His precise measure. Some of these accounts were compiled in a strange book called the *Shi'ur Qomah*, the "Measure of the Body," in the sixth century C.E.:

> His body is like aquamarine. His radiance scintillates, awesome from within the darkness. Dense clouds surround him. All the angels of the Presence pour themselves out before him as water pouring from a pitcher. His tongue extends from one end of the universe to the other. The width of his forehead is 130 million parasangs; on it are written seventy letters. The black of his right eye is 11,500 parasangs, and so on the left. From his right shoulder to his left shoulder is 160 million parasangs. . . . his palms are each 40 million parasangs. His toes are 100 million parasangs, each one 20 million. Therefore he is called "the great, mighty, and awesome God."
>
> But then Metatron told me how to calculate the parasangs. What is their measure? Each parasang is three

miles, each mile is 10,000 cubits, each cubit is two
spans—measured according to God's span, which spans
the entire universe.

Although the specificity of language in passages such as this
one verges on idolatry, the intention is quite the opposite. The
exuberance of the hyperbole explodes the very idea of measure.
This is ecstatic poetry, not scientific observation.

One technique that these astral adventurers used to put
themselves into a trance was to sing long, droning, repetitive
songs. Some of these so-called *Heikhalot* hymns later found
their way into the liturgy—Gershom Scholem translates one
called "Song of the Angels," which some Hasidic Jews still in-
tone as a Sabbath morning prayer to this day. Needless to say,
the following excerpt is just a tiny fragment of it:

> *Excellence and faithfulness—are His who lives forever*
> *Understanding and blessing—are His who lives forever*
> *Grandeur and greatness—are His who lives forever*
> *Cognition and expression—are His who lives forever*
> *Magnificence and majesty—are His who lives forever*
> *Counsel and strength—are His who lives forever*
> *Luster and brilliance—are His who lives forever*
> *Grace and benevolence—are His who lives forever*
> *Purity and goodness—are His who lives forever*
> *Unity and honor—are His who lives forever*

The *Merkabah* and *Heikhalot* visions may be majestic and
poetic. They may be rich in magical lore (all those incantations,
amulets, and secret names had great practical utility for sorcer-

ers and healers—*theurgy*, or magic, makes use of the signatures of objects or beings, their names, in other words, to manipulate or control them, and these mystics had in their possession countless secret names of God Himself). Yet by the year 1000 c.e. (the end of the Geonic Era*), most of these ecstatic practices had passed well out of the mainstream of Judaism. The metaphysical visions of the *Merkabah* and *Heikhalot* mystics, exclusively focused as they were on personal communion with God, had little to add to such worldly concerns as ethics, the obligations of the community, and a sense of national destiny, all of them equally important to Judaism—if not more so. By contrast, as we will see, the Kabbalah that would develop in the Middle Ages contained strong ethical and messianic components that affected Judaism as it was practiced and lived day to day.

### BERESHIT (CREATION) MYSTICISM
### AND THE SEFER YEZIRAH

One mystical text from the rabbinic era, the *Sefer Yezirah* ("The Book of Creation"), would have a decisive, outsized impact on Judaism for centuries to come. A short (less than two thousand words in its most extensive edition, one version fits neatly onto a single page), enigmatic document of unknown origins (most scholars date it from the first or second century c.e., but as-

---

*658–1000 c.e., when the center of Jewish intellectual life moved to Babylonia. *Gaon* is the Hebrew word for majesty or excellence; its plural is *geonim*. The *geonim* were the heads of the great schools; the term came to be used as an honorific for any great Talmud scholar.

sume it contains later additions), it is the best-known example of *Bereshit* mysticism. Written in a terse Hebrew that is stylistically distinct from any other writings of its era, dense with abstruse formulas, numbers, and cryptic sayings, the *Sefer Yezirah* tells how God created the universe using thirty-two "secret paths" of wisdom. These paths comprise the twenty-two Hebrew consonants plus something called the ten *Sefirot*.

This is not a metaphor. The *Sefer Yezirah* declares that the ultimate essence of creation, its underlying atomic structure—its substrate, as it were—quite literally consists of Hebrew letters and the *Sefirot*. "Ten *Sefirot* of Nothingness: ten and not nine, ten and not eleven," the *Sefer Yezirah* intones. "Understand with Wisdom, and be wise with Understanding. Discern with them, probe from them, and know, think and depict."

The Torah told the Jewish people that the world was created with ten divine utterances ("Let there be light," etc.); it supplied them with the Ten Commandments to regulate our behavior. The *Sefer Yezirah* gave them ten *Sefirot: Keter* (crown), *Hokhmah* (wisdom), *Binah* (understanding), *Hesed* (love), *Gevurah* (strength), *Tif'eret* (beauty), *Netzah* (victory), *Hod* (splendor), *Yesod* (foundation), and *Shekhinah* (presence). The origins of the word are uncertain, but it seems to be related to the Hebrew words for book (*sefer*), number (*sephar*), and "telling" (*sippur*).

So exactly what are the *Sefirot*? Neoplatonic emanations from the Godhead? Manifestations of divine power? A set of lesser deities, à la Gnosticism? Medieval quantum physics? Yes, no, maybe, and none of the above—the *Sefer Yezirah* never really gets around to offering a concise, systematic definition of them. As the great modern Kabbalah scholar Aryeh Kaplan remarks wryly in the introduction to his translation and commentary, "if the author meant to be obscure, he was eminently successful."

Even so, this notion of creation from letters and numbers—and especially from these ten mysterious divine manifestations known as *Sefirot*—will prove to be absolutely key concepts in the Kabbalah as it would emerge in Provence and Germany in the eleven hundreds. The major kabbalistic texts of the eleven hundreds, the *Sefer-ha-Bahir* and the twelve hundreds, the *Zohar*, would have a great deal more to say about the *Sefirot*, as we shall see in the next chapter when we delve into them in detail. But the *Sefer Yezirah* was their source.

A bibliography of commentaries on the *Sefer Yezirah* would contain scores of entries, by a veritable "who's who" of Jewish mystics—Judah Halevi (1075–1143), Eleazar of Worms (1165–1230), Abraham Abulafia (1240–1291), and Moses Cordovero (1522–1570), to name only a few. But it's important to remember that the *Sefirot* can never be explained with anything like the transparency and precision of a coherent philosophical system. They are neither pure ideas nor material phenomena: they are a revelation of the mystical unity of creation, as beautiful and elusive as a glimpse of a heavenly chariot or a celestial palace. Though they can be described in words up to a point, the *Sefirot* can only be truly apprehended in meditation. For now, perhaps the best way to describe them is as sacred emanations, aspects of a single, divine source. In the sixteenth century, Moses Cordovero would compare them to a set of translucent, colored vessels. As water (the divine essence) flows through them, it seems to change its color, though its essence remains the same. In the words of the *Sefer Yezirah:*

> Their end is imbedded in their beginning, and their be-
> ginning in their end, like a flame attached to a burning
> coal. Know, think and depict that the Creator is One,
> there is no other, and before One what do you count?

What's fascinating about the *Sefer Yezirah* is how many levels it works on at the same time. It is a work of revelation—its author is reporting a personal vision. But its extensive iterations of Hebrew letter and vowel combinations, its lengthy categorizations of divine attributes, its interminable catalogs of physiological, astrological, and calendar correspondences ("Saturn in the Universe, Friday in the Year, the left nostril in the Soul, male and female") are not just descriptions of the organizing principles of creation, like something you would find in a physics textbook today—they are guided meditations. There can be little doubt that the *Sefer Yezirah* was written first and foremost as a handbook for meditators. But it doesn't end there.

These contemplative exercises have a practical purpose—they are explicitly designed to focus and strengthen the concentration of initiates, so they will be able to perform works of creation for themselves. For the *Sefer Yezirah* is also a manual, a how-to book for would-be wonder-workers. Once we have a deep enough understanding of the secrets of creation, it implicitly declares, there is nothing preventing us from using the same tools that God did—words and numbers—to make creations of our own: it's simply a matter of application. No wonder the

Kabbalah was considered to be so dangerous! We see here the roots of the legend of Faust—and of the awe with which atomic physicists and genetic engineers are regarded today.

The Talmud tells us that the fourth-century C.E. sage Rava, the founder of the Babylonian academy in Mechuza, and Rav Zeira, known as the "Saint of Babylon," meditated for three years on the *Sefer Yezirah*. Once they had mastered it, they created a calf and slaughtered it. Then they lost their powers and had to work for three more years before they got them back again. The Talmud also tells us that Rava once "created a man" and sent him on an errand to Rav Zeira. When Rav Zeira saw that this man lacked the power of speech he realized it was a golem, a magical android (see below), and ordered it to return to the dust.

---

### So You Want to Make a Golem

It's challenging enough just to read and understand the *Sefer Yezirah*. Then you have to put the very complicated procedures that it teaches into practice. This requires discipline, patience, wisdom, intelligence, and almost unimaginable spiritual strength. But it's not out of the realm of possibility.

Rabbi Eleazar of Worms's commentary on the *Sefer Yezirah* includes detailed instructions for making a golem, an artificial human being. Before you begin, you'll need to memorize a bewildering number of verbal formulae—and to be able to utter tens of thousands of Hebrew phonemes and phrases in the correct order and without making any mistakes. Then you and your partners (you should never create a golem by yourself!) should purify yourselves and dress in clean white vestments. You'll need a sufficient supply of virgin soil, taken from a place that's never been dug, and fresh springwater that has never been poured into a vessel of any sort. After you mix the soil and water and knead it together, it's time to get to work. Taking care to breathe properly and to make the right head movements, you'll have to combine each Hebrew letter and vowel with each of the consonants of the tetragrammaton (the four-letter name of God, YHWH, that pious Jews are forbidden to pronounce out loud—instead they pronounce them as *Adonai,* or "Lord"), while meditating on the parts of the body. Depending on how you combine the vowels and which sequences you use (not all rabbis agree about this—Rabbi Abraham Abulafia's instructions for golem-making, for example, require tens of thousands more combinations than Rabbi Eleazar's), the entire process should take between seven and thirty-five hours.

When you have finished, the golem you have created will only be a mental image. But that doesn't mean that he has to remain in your mind. You can project yourself into this mental construct and use it as a vehicle to ascend to astral realms—or you can transfer it into the clay form that you mixed and bring it to life in the real world. If you don't want to create a whole man, you can create just a single limb or organ—a useful tool in the practice of medicine.

One of the best-known legends about a golem takes place in the late fifteen hundreds, when Rabbi Judah Loew created one to protect the Jews of Prague from a pogrom. When the creature went out of control, threatening to slaughter all of the gentiles in the city, the rabbi undid his magic. The story was actually adapted from a popular legend about Loew's contemporary, Rabbi Elijah of Chelm; Loew became its hero only in the late eighteenth century.

To this day the *Golem* lies in the uppermost part of the synagogue of Prague, covered with cobwebs that have spun from wall to wall to encase the whole arcade so that it should be hidden from all human eyes, especially pregnant wives in the women's section. No one is permitted to touch the cobwebs, for anyone who does so dies. Even the oldest congregants no longer remember the *Golem*. However, Zvi the Sage, the grandson of the Maharal, still deliberates whether it is proper to include the *Golem* in a *minyan* or in a company for the saying of grace.

The lines quoted above are from Ruth Wisse's translation of the great Yiddish writer I. L. Peretz's short story "The Golem," which appeared in 1893.

The golem has been ubiquitous in popular literature since Mary Shelley's *Frankenstein* was published in 1818. He has turned up recently in Arnold Schwarzenegger's *Terminator* movies and novels like Frances Sherwood's *The Book of Splendor*, *The Golems of Gotham* by Thane Rosenbaum, Cynthia Ozick's *The Puttermesser Papers*, and Michael Chabon's award-winning novel *The Amazing Adventures of Kavalier and Clay.*

---

EARLY KABBALAH

As the first millennium drew near its close, the notion of *gilgul* (see page 32), or the transmigration of souls, was beginning to take hold in various Jewish circles in the Middle East. Soon it would travel to Europe. If there were fewer ascents to the chariot and the palaces than there had been, many rabbis were us-

---
— How Come? —
---

*Since When Do Jews Believe in Reincarnation?*

The Greek philosopher Pythagoras believed that souls are "recycled" through various incarnations, human or animal, until they are pure enough to return to their source among the gods. The idea was foreign to Judaism until the eighth century C.E., when the Karaites (an antirabbinical sect) adopted it. The tenth-century scholar Saadia scornfully refuted their ideas as "nonsense and stupidity" in his *Book of Beliefs and Opinions*.

The idea reemerged in the twelve hundreds and within a few generations had taken root in kabbalistic thinking, perhaps because it offers a clear answer to the question: How does a good God permit innocent children to suffer? Because they are not as innocent as they appear: their souls have sinned in other lives.

According to Rabbi Luria and his followers, souls originated as sparks from the primal Adam (who contained the souls of every person who would ever be created)—but they were polluted by Adam's original sin, as well as the sins they committed in their own incarnations. Until the Messiah comes, souls will wander continuously from body to body—into good men if they are relatively pure, into animals or inanimate objects if they are especially corrupt. While souls that have transmigrated into humans are blissfully unaware of their former state, human souls that have sinned so severely that they are forced to reside in animals suffer terribly.

Another idea that the Safed kabbalists promoted was *ibbur* or "impregnation." If a purified soul had neglected to perform all the *mitzvot,* or good deeds, that were required of it in its lifetime, for example, it might be permitted to borrow a living body so that it could make good that omission; a visiting good soul can help a weaker host soul fulfill its own obligations. According to Lurianic kabbalism, a body can hold up to two foreign souls—provided that they share the same point of origin in the primal Adam (i.e., a spark that was emitted from Adam's stomach can't share a body with a spark from Adam's eye).

Practical kabbalists know how to find the mark on your forehead that reveals what class of soul you have, how many transmigrations it has endured, and what it still needs to do to be purified. A wandering soul that's so evil that it's not allowed to transmigrate is a dybbuk. Although belief in demonic possession is as timeless as mental illness, the term is not from the Talmud or the Kabbalah. In fact, it doesn't appear in print until the seventeenth century (*dibbuk me-ru'ah ra'ah* means "a cleavage of an evil spirit" in Yiddish). When such a soul invades a living body it has to be exorcised by a *baal shem* (a "master of the name," a wonder-worker and/or healer).

---

ing sacred names to work wonders and devising more and more intricate and ingenious *Gematria* to explain the Torah.

In the eleventh century, the Spanish rabbi Bahya ibn Paquda wrote *Hovot ha-Levavot,* a book that instructed pious Jews in how to infuse obedience to the law with impassioned spirituality and mystical aspiration. The book would be widely influential throughout Europe as *Duties of the Heart* when, in the mid–eleven hundreds, it was translated from Arabic into Hebrew in Provence, which had become a virtual petri dish of kabbalistic development. But it was in Germany, not Provence, that the classic European Kabbalah first began to develop.

The Pious Ones of Germany: The *Hassidei Ashkenaz*

*Merkabah* mysticism (and the magical secrets of the *Sefer Yezirah*) first traveled to Europe in the ninth century C.E. They were brought there by an astonishing, semimythical figure named Aaron of Baghdad. Aaron had been banished from Babylonia, the story goes, for the sin of making something exalted serve a base purpose—he had enchanted a lion and harnessed it to a millstone to punish it for killing the donkey that had been turning the stone. While sojourning in Italy, Aaron met Rabbi Moses ben Kalonymides, a famous liturgical poet, and "transmitted his secrets to him." Those secrets would travel farther north later that century, when the Kalonymides family immigrated to Germany.

Jewish traders, with their valuable contacts throughout the Levant, had initially been the beneficiaries of royal protection when they settled in the Rhineland; for a few generations they had enjoyed relative peace and prosperity. But this idyll came to an abrupt and terrible end when the peasant armies of the Crusaders began to target the Jewish communities. Starting in 1096, when the Jewish communities of Mainz, Speyer, and Worms were plundered, and continuing for the next two centuries, the Jews in the Rhineland not only had to endure periodic outbreaks of violence, but with the establishment of Crusader colonies along the coast of the Mediterranean, they would lose their monopoly on Middle Eastern trade. Staggered by their loss of life, liberty, status, and wealth, some German Jews began to gravitate toward a new movement, the *Hasidei Ashkenaz,* or the Pious Ones of Germany (this movement is not related to modern Hasidism, which began in the sixteen hundreds).

Its best-known spiritual leaders were Samuel the Hasid (birth and death unknown), his son, Jehudah the Hasid of Worms (1150–1217), and his disciple and relative Eleazar. All of them were members of the Kalonymides family; many of their writings were collected in a book called the *Sefer Hasidim*.

The *Hasidei Ashkenaz* combined the *Merkabah* mysticism that their ancestors had learned from Aaron of Baghdad with Jewish and German folk beliefs in demons and witches, Roman Stoicism, and innumerable other occult and pietistic influences. The result was a strange hybrid. They embraced ecstatic visions but imposed an uncompromising devotion to biblical law; they believed in vampires, werewolves, and sorcery but were also obsessed with *kiddush ha-shem*, a Hebrew phrase which is literally translated as "the sanctification of the divine name," but which implies a willingness to embrace martyrdom—a fate that was all too familiar for the German Jews of the twelfth century. Eleazar of Worms would witness the murders of his own children during one Crusader massacre.

The Hasid had access to immense power through his knowledge of magic. Eleazar, for example, was reputed to have traveled on clouds—he walked with a limp because he once fell off of one; his instructions for creating a golem are cited elsewhere in this chapter. Even so, the Hasids lived lives of uncompromising austerity. It's worth noting, however, that unlike so many ascetic Christian movements of the Middle Ages, the Hasids did not renounce sex—they had a high regard for the importance of healthy marital relations, even if their love of God offered more intense satisfactions. The following passage from Eleazar of Worms illustrates this graphically, if not pornographically:

The Root of Love [of God]: It is to love God when the soul is overflowing with love, and is bound with the bonds of love in great happiness. This happiness drives away from a person's heart the pleasures of the body and the enjoyment of worldly things. This great love and joy overcomes his heart and makes him think constantly how he could fulfill the wish of God. The enjoyment of his children and wife become like nothing compared with the immense love of God. [What he feels is] more than like a young man who did not have sexual intercourse with a woman for a long time, and he craves her and desires her and his heart is burning to be with her, and because of his great love and desire when he has intercourse with her his semen shoots from him like an arrow and his enjoyment is supreme. All this is like nothing compared with the following of God's will.

By the beginning of the twelfth century, most German Jews despaired of ever being able to participate in German culture again, nor could they repose much faith in conventional Judaism's increasingly hollow-sounding promises of divine favor and protection. The Hasidim offered an intriguing alternative—surrendering any expectations of earthly happiness, they would meet the hostility and manifest injustices of the world with unstinting saintliness.

In his recent book *Heavenly Powers: Unraveling the Secrets of the Kabbalah*, the historian Neil Silberman argues that the piety of the Hasids cloaked an implicit radical critique of the economic and political injustices suffered by the Jews; that their mysticism was really politics by other means. In contrast, Gershom Scholem's extensive writings about the *Hasidei Ashkenaz* play down the historical circumstances of the German Jews, noting that the same era saw a marked rise in Christian mysticism as well. "Three things above all others go to make the true *Hasid*," Scholem writes. "Ascetic renunciation of the things of this world; complete serenity of mind; and an altruism grounded in principle and driven to extremes."

A likely contribution of Christianity to the ethos of the *Hasidei Ashkenaz* is their obsession with penance. Not only did the Hasids carefully codify appropriate penances for sins like adultery and violating the Sabbath; they tormented themselves to atone for even their involuntary sins. Scholem relates the following story from the *Sefer Hasidim:*

> A *Hasid* was in the habit of sleeping on the floor in summer, among the fleas, and placing his feet into a bucket with water in winter, until they froze into one lump with the ice. A pupil asked him: Why do you do that? Why, since man is responsible for his life, do you expose yourself to certain danger? The *Hasid* replied: It is true that I have not committed any deadly sin, and though I am surely guilty of lighter transgressions there is no need for me to expose myself to such tortures. But it is said in the *Midrash* that the Messiah is suffering for our sins, as it is said (Isaiah LIII, 5): "he is wounded for our transgressions," and those who are truly just take sufferings upon themselves for their generation.

The *Hasidei Ashkenaz* also incorporated elements of Neoplatonism and Gnosticism. As they saw it, God was present in creation but largely detached from it. The Hasid's goal was the *kavod,* God's glory, visible atop Ezekiel's chariot. As the *Sefer Hasidim* puts it, "when a person's soul leaves the body, it bears evil corresponding to its sin. If [the person] was perfectly righteous, the soul ascends to the Throne of Glory and adheres to the Upper Throne."

For the most part, the theology of the Hasids is a mishmash of poorly understood, frequently contradictory ideas. Gershom Scholem, with his characteristic asperity, notes "the lack of talent, peculiar to the Hasidim, for precisely worded abstract thought." But if he is frustrated by their lack of intellectual rigor and embarrassed by their superstitions, he can't disguise his admiration for their heartfelt efforts to fuse the mythical, the mystical, the metaphysical, and the moral. The Hasids had brought mysticism back down to earth, advancing a comprehensible (if unattainable for most people) ideal for religious conduct: absolute, uncompromising righteousness, above and beyond the requirements of the law, based on the conviction that everyone could participate in the work of redemption. Although their ideas are almost always described as deeply pessimistic, the Hasids firmly believed that what we do in the world below has everything to do with what will happen in the world to come: this notion would become a key component of Kabbalah as it continued to develop in southern Europe.

### Provence and the *Sefer-ha-Bahir*

Meanwhile in Provence, starting in the early tenth century, a radical new idea had taken hold among the Christians of southern France: the Cathar heresy (by the end of the eleven hundreds it would also be known as the Albigensian heresy). The Cathari (the Greek word for "puritans") believed that the world was created by Satan, who was masquerading as the God of the Old Testament. By renouncing all sensual pleasures, ceasing to procreate, and most of all, by repudiating the Catholic Church, the Cathari hoped to win favor with the true God, the creator of the heavens and the celestial realms, and reunite their souls with Him. This shocking challenge to Catholic orthodoxy brought onto the Cathari the repression that was usually reserved for the Jews. Their venturesome spirit (not to mention their Gnostic tendencies) undoubtedly influenced their mystically inclined Jewish neighbors.

Late in the eleven hundreds, the *Sefer-ha-Bahir* ("The Book of Brightness") began to circulate in southern France. Scholars have argued about the *Bahir*'s origins for centuries. Its language, content, and some of its imagery suggest that at least parts of it are very old—as old or older than the *Sefer Yezirah*—but it reflects many newer influences as well. For a long time it was wrongly attributed to the well-known Provençal rabbi Isaac the Blind (1160–1236). More likely it was a revision of a much older text that had traveled to France via the *Hasidei Ashkenaz* in Germany.

Regardless of where it came from, its impact would be enormous. This was the first work of Jewish mysticism to bring together the notions of the *Sefirot* (the ten attributes of God first described in the *Sefer Yezirah*), reincarnation, and human involvement in the repair of the cosmos—the central ideas of the classic Kabbalah. Along with commentary on the shapes of Hebrew letters and *Gematria,* it contains midrashic dialogues among Talmudic sages (some of them historical figures, some of them fictional characters) as well as stories and parables. The *Bahir* has much more to say about the *Sefirot* than the *Sefer Yezirah* did; it describes them as the media through which divine energies are conducted into and out of the world.

Unlike the chariot and the palaces of the early mystics, the ten *Sefirot* aren't something that you can travel to. But in one essential way, they're not that different—they can only be grasped in the mind, as an object of sustained meditation. Any two-dimensional, static representation of them would be misleading. They are constantly in motion, and they take their meaning from their constantly shifting relationships with each other. Nevertheless, one of the most enduring metaphoric descriptions of the *Sefirot* first appears in the *Bahir*—the image of the tree of life. The ten *Sefirot* are nodes; the branches and trunk of the tree map out their interrelationships. From the *Bahir*:

> *What is this tree that you mentioned?*
> *He said: It represents the Powers of the Blessed Holy One, one*
> *above the other.*
> *Just like a tree brings forth fruit through water, so the Blessed*
> *Holy One increases the Powers of the Tree through water.*
> *What is the water of the Blessed Holy One?*
> *It is wisdom. It is the souls of the righteous. They fly from the*
> *fountain to the great pip [seeded fruit], ascend and attach*
> *themselves to the Tree.*

Central to the *Bahir* is its emphasis on the role of reincarnation—formerly, as we have seen, a fringe notion in Judaism.

Interestingly enough, reincarnation plays a major role in the Cathar heresy as well—but to a very different purpose. The Cathari regarded the transmigration of souls as one of Satan's cruelest tricks—they believed that the endless recirculation of souls from one incarnation to another prevented them from returning to their proper home in heaven. If the Cathari inspired this new interest in reincarnation, the *Bahir* gives it a much more positive spin. There reincarnation is the process by which souls are purified in preparation for their ultimate return to God. When good people suffer, the sage Rahumai explains in one of the *Bahir*'s dialogues, it is to atone for sins committed in a previous life; he suggests that up to a thousand reincarnations might be necessary before those sins are sufficiently purged.

The authors or compilers of the *Bahir* gave us an earth and heaven that are intimately interconnected. God manifests himself in the world both through the *Sefirot* and the form and content of the Torah. Evil is not an alien principle to God, as it is for the Cathari—it is what occurs when the divine powers that are manifested on earth through the *Sefirot* fall out of balance, when there is too much *Gevurah* (judgment and power) and not enough *Hesed* (compassion and love). By living an ethical life, the *Bahir* declares, people can help to redress that imbalance.

Shortly after the *Bahir* appeared in Provence in the mid-twelfth century, three important rabbis claimed to have received visits from the prophet Elijah. They were Abraham ben Isaac, chief of the rabbinical court in Narbonne, his son-in-law Abraham ben David of Posquieres, and Jacob "the Nazirite" of

Lunel (Nazirites, from the Hebrew *Nazir*, "consecrated one," were ascetic rabbis who were supported by their communities). The content of Elijah's message has never been disclosed; most historians suspect that it had something to do with the use of the *Sefirot* in prayer and meditation.

# THE RISE OF KABBALAH:
# THE *ZOHAR* AND RABBI ISAAC LURIA

*I, Rabbi Isaac of Akko, was contemplating, according to the method I received from the great one of his generation—great in humility, the wisdom of Kabbalah, philosophy, and the science of permutation of letters. He insisted that I set the ten* Sefirot *in front of me, as it is written: "I set YHVH before me always." I saw them today above my head like a pillar, with their feet on my head and their heads high above, beyond all the four worlds: emanation, creation, formation, and actualization. As long as I was contemplating this ladder—the name of the Blessed Holy One—I saw my soul cleaving to* Ein Sof.

—ISAAC OF AKKO 1250–1350 C.E.

## FROM PROVENCE TO GERONA, SPAIN

In the mid-thirteenth century, Abraham Maimonides, the leader of the Egyptian Jewish community and the son of Moses Maimonides (1135–1204),* wrote a treatise in Arabic

---

*Often called "the second Moses," the elder Maimonides, author of the *Mishneh Torah* and *The Guide for the Perplexed,* was perhaps the greatest Jewish philosopher who ever lived, renowned among Christians and Muslims as well as Jews for his efforts to reconcile Aristotelian science with biblical revelation. He is often referred to as Rambam, the Hebrew acronym for his full name, Rabbi Moses ben Maimon.

called *Kifāyat al-'Abidīn,* which espoused an ethically oriented "Jewish Sufism." "The ways of the ancient saints of Israel," the son of the Rambam regretfully declared, "have now become the practice of the Sufis of Islam." Although there is scant evidence that his book directly influenced the development of Kabbalah, it suggests how much mysticism was in the air. It also provides a memorable illustration of the fact that Judaism and Islam have not always been at odds.

By the twelve hundreds, the word *Kabbalah* had come to have a special meaning, beyond the literal "tradition." Within a small but steadily expanding community of European Jewish rabbis, it was understood to refer specifically to mystical interpretations of the Torah—particularly those relying on *Gematria* and other esoteric algorithms, and especially to the *Sefirot* and the special prayers and meditations associated with them. Isaac the Blind, the son of Rabbi Abraham ben David (one of the Provençal rabbis who claimed to have been visited by Elijah), would attract disciples all across southern Europe. Known as "the Hasid" (and by the honorific "father of the Kabbalah"), he was the first to establish the notion of *Ein Sof* ("the Infinite"), the supernal "nothingness" of the Godhead—the unchanging source of the Sefirotic emanations (this concept will be discussed in greater detail in the following pages).

Starting around 1209, the Roman Catholic Church began its "Albigensian Crusade"—a singularly brutal attempt to quash the Cathar heresy once and for all. In Provence, tens of thousands of Cathars were slaughtered as a full-scale Inquisition began. Inevitably, there were attacks against the Jews as well. Many of Isaac's students fled from France to Spain where, to his consternation, some of them began to teach Kabbalah openly, and even to publish their writings. "What is written cannot be kept in the closet," he rebuked them. "Often these things are lost or the owners die and the writings fall into the hands of fools or scoffers, and the name of heaven is thus profaned."

Over the course of the twelve hundreds the Catalonian town of Gerona, located between the Pyrenees and Barcelona, would become the most important center of Jewish mystical thought in Europe. Azriel of Gerona (1160–1238) wrote an influential commentary on the *Sefer Yezirah;* Azriel's student Nachmanides (1194–1270) would become the most important Jewish legal and religious authority of his day. Nachmanides's fame was such that in 1263 King James I of Aragon ordered him to engage in a public debate with a converted Jew named Pablo Christiani about the merits of Judaism versus Christianity. Although the king rewarded him with three hundred gold coins for his performance, he was eventually exiled as an enemy of Catholicism; he finished his life in Jerusalem. Although not a kabbalist himself, his early involvement with it lent the movement tremendous credibility.

## THE ECSTATIC KABBALAH OF ABRAHAM ABULAFIA

Born in Spain in 1240 (he died around 1291), the great kabbalist Abraham Abulafia was deeply learned in philosophy and natural science. Though he admired the sober, systematic rationalism of the elder Maimonides, Abulafia is best known as a visionary, the leading exponent of the "ecstatic Kabbalah." As far as Abulafia was concerned, there was no conflict between their very different methods.

Maimonides's reason and logic could only take one so far, Abulafia maintained. Seeking a way to "unseal the soul, to untie the knots which bind it," so that it can "return to [its] origin, which is one without any duality," he contrived *Hokhmath ha-Tseruf,* the "science of the combination of letters," by which anyone can experience revelation firsthand. It was the inevitable next step on the path to enlightenment.

One of Abulafia's students left behind this frequently quoted testimony:

> He taught me the method of the permutations and combinations of letters and the mysticism of numbers and the other "Paths of the Book *Yesirah.*" In each path he had me wander for two weeks until each form had been engraven in my heart, and so he led me on for four months or so and then ordered me to "efface" everything.
>
> He used to tell me: "My son, it is not the intention that you come to a stop with some finite or given form, even though it be of the highest order. Much rather is this the "Path of the Names": The less understandable they are, the higher their order, until you arrive at the activity of a force which is no longer in your control, but rather your reason and your thought is in its control.

Onerous mental gymnastics, endless repetitions of meaningless phrases, special postures and breathing exercises combined to short-circuit conventional thought patterns and alter the texture of consciousness—Abulafia's "science" sounds remarkably like the meditational practices of yogis and Sufis (it is not inconceivable that the resemblance is more than coincidental, as he traveled widely throughout Muslim Spain and the Middle East). At any rate, the results Abulafia promised (and by all accounts delivered) to assiduous users of his method were unabashedly spectacular, even psychedelic: "Thy whole body will be seized by an extremely strong trembling, so that thou wilt think that surely thou art about to die, because thy soul, overjoyed with its knowledge, will leave thy body," he declared. "And be thou ready at this moment consciously to choose death, and then thou shalt know that thou hast come far enough to receive the influx."

As we have seen, magicians had long used the divine names as tools. Abulafia's manipulation of them bears some resemblance to magical practice, but in fact he disdained sorcery and the conjuring of spirits; he condemned them in no uncertain terms as contrary to the spirit of true mysticism:

> I have found in one of the books, whose title I would like not to mention: "Whoever wants to bring a woman to him so that she will love him, let him pronounce the name of WHW YLY SYT 'LM, frontward and backward seven times, in the night of Wednesday, during the first hour of night, which is the time of Saturn, and let him conjure Qaftziel, that is the angel presiding over that planet, by that name. At that time let him write four names on a parchment of a deer, without interrupting the writing by any speech. Then, let him put the amulet on his neck as an amulet and then the woman, whose name

and the name of her father he has pronounced, will love
him a great love, by the virtue of that name." Similar
things I have found in great numbers, and they are almost
infinite; and these things have spread and reached the
hands of great Rabbis. . . . Those and those like them, together with their Rabbis, have been caught by the
demons and their eyes have been darkened, and their
hearts blinded, and they have been brought to madness
and death.

Most likely Abulafia is parodying a typical love spell, but as you
will see in chapter 5 of this book, which covers magic and superstition, he was hardly exaggerating.

Abulafia accepted only mature, well-balanced Torah scholars
as students, and even then he insisted that they begin their con-
templations in a temperate mode, starting with what he called
the "Path of the *Sefiroth.*" Only when they had mastered the
"rabbinical" Kabbalah would he permit them to proceed down
the "Path of Names" that led to his "ecstatic" or "prophetic"
Kabbalah.

Despite his evident learning, piety, and doctrinal conservatism, almost none of Abulafia's innumerable treatises, proph-
esies, memoirs, and other writings found their way into print
until his rediscovery by scholars in the nineteenth century.
Gershom Scholem singles out Abulafia as "the least popular of
all the great Kabbalists." While Abulafia evinced an undoubted
talent for controversy during his lifetime, posterity's evident
distaste for him might well be because his methods worked all
too well. "Abulafia gives you a one-way ticket to outer space,"
the well-known meditation teacher Rabbi Jonathan Omer-

Man dryly observes, in Rodger Kamenetz's *Stalking Elijah: Adventures with Today's Jewish Mystical Masters*. A successful follower of Abulafia's "Path of Names," Gershom Scholem writes, "is, so to speak, his own Messiah, at least for the brief period of his ecstatical experience."

A thousand years before Abulafia was born, the Talmud had warned would-be visionaries about the grim fates that awaited the three rabbis who ventured into the "orchard" unprepared. Abulafia's own experiences provide something of a cautionary tale. In 1280, seized with the conviction that he was the Messiah, Abulafia traveled to Rome to convert the Pope, Nicholas III, to Judaism. In doing so, he ignored the warnings he had received that the Pope—far from agreeing to meet with him—had issued orders to have him burned at the stake. Miraculously, the Pope died the night before Abulafia arrived. He was imprisoned by the Franciscans but they released him unharmed after a month. Abulafia's good luck eventually ran its course. He would end his days in exile, condemned as a charlatan by the rabbinical authority Simon Adret of Barcelona (1235–1310).

## THE PROBLEM OF EVIL: THE "LEFT" EMANATION

While Abulafia was pursuing his eccentric course, the brothers Jacob and Isaac ha-Kohen were developing their theory of the "Left Emanation" (a sort of "through-the-looking-glass" version of the *Sefirot* in which evil comes into the world by a different series of emanations than the ones that bring in God). Citing a rare manuscript he had seen in Provence, which supposedly originated in Damascus, Isaac ha-Kohen revealed that this world was not God's first creation—there were at least three previous ones, but those worlds had been annihilated because of the incorrigible evil of their inhabitants. Despite those earlier purges, ha-Kohen claimed, in his *Treatise on the Left Emanation,* the demoness Lilith and her husband Samael, the "great prince and great king over all the demons," still found their way into our own world, where they enjoy considerable sway.

> This is the account of Lilith which was received by the Sages in the *Secret Knowledge of the Palaces.* The Matron Lilith is the mate of Samael. Both of them were born at the same hour in the image of Adam and Eve, intertwined in each other. Asmodeus the great king of the demons has as a mate the Lesser (younger) Lilith, daughter of the king whose name is Qafsefoni. The name of his mate is Mehetabel daughter of Matred, and their daughter is Lilith.
>
> This is the exact text of what is written in *The Chapters of the Lesser Palaces* as we have received it, word for word and letter for letter. And the scholars of this wisdom possess a very profound tradition from the ancients. They found it stated in those *Chapters* that Samael, the great prince of them all, grew exceedingly jealous of Asmodeus the king of the demons because of this Lilith who is called Lilith the Maiden (the young). She is in the form of a beautiful woman from her head to her waist. But from the waist down she is burning fire—like mother like daughter.

The implications are profound: If all of creation emanates directly from God, then evil must be a part of the divine substance. But that would mean that God is not entirely good. On the other hand, if God is not the source of evil and has no control over it, then that sharply limits His power, leading to the heretical conclusions of Gnosticism or polytheism. The ha-Kohens' "solution" is more mythological than philosophical, and it fails to avoid either pitfall. As we will see, this issue would be taken up again in the Lurianic Kabbalah that was to arise in Safed, Palestine, some two and a half centuries later.

In the meantime, Abraham Abulafia's student Joseph Gikatilla (1248–1305) continued to develop the theoretical framework for the *Sefirot,* working closely with Moses de Leon, who by the end of the thirteenth century was already editing (and, as we shall soon see, most likely writing) the *Zohar,* kabbalism's greatest text. Azriel of Gerona, in his turn, produced a body of work that seamlessly incorporated the language and categories of Neoplatonism into Kabbalah. As the thirteenth century drew to a close, Kabbalah was beginning to be treated as a form of philosophy, and the *Sefirot* played a larger and larger role in it. It is past time that we discuss them in depth.

## TEN DIVINE EMANATIONS: THE *SEFIROT*

By the beginning of the thirteen hundreds, the idea of the *Sefirot*—the ten "emanations" from God that channel divine influences into and out of our world—had been evolving for hundreds of years. From their enigmatic origin in the *Sefer*

*Yezirah* as the "ten *Sefirot* of Nothingness," they had at last come to resemble something like a fully articulated metaphysical system.

But this is misleading. For all of their apparent precision and subtlety, most descriptions of the *Sefirot* are rife with contradictions. Sometimes they seem to suggest a pantheistic conception of God, in which everything in our world is literally compounded from a divine substance; at other times, they suggest a Gnostic or polytheistic universe, in which hierarchies of greater and lesser gods and demons preside over a series of greater and lesser worlds. Even so, the Kabbalists insisted not only that the *Sefirot* were compatible with traditional monotheism, but also that they were a profound expression of it. The "oneness" of these ten emanations is a sacred mystery, as ineffable as the oneness of the Christian Trinity. Volumes could be written (indeed many already have been) addressing this theological conundrum, but for now it will be sufficient to note, borrowing Gershom Scholem's words, that, far from representing a contribution to philosophy, "the doctrine of the *Sefirot* was the main tenet clearly *dividing* the Kabbalah from Jewish philosophy" [emphasis added].

But if the doctrine of the *Sefirot* falls short of providing an internally consistent, intellectually coherent account of the nature of God, they nonetheless go far in showing how we creatures perceive and relate to our Creator—and in that sense they can speak to us just as eloquently today as they did to the kabbalists of a thousand years ago. Perhaps the most useful way for us to think of the *Sefirot* is as a metaphorical representation of religious experience.

Much of the following account of the *Sefirot* is indebted to
the writings of the contemporary Kabbalah scholar, Arthur
Green, particularly his book *Ehyeh: A Kabbalah for Tomorrow*.
In his words:

> The *Sefirot* are stages of spiritual "ascent," going up the
> ladder of abstraction until one is fully lost or absorbed in
> the mystery of Oneness. They are also rungs of "descent,"
> the return to this "lower" world of daily reality. Kabbalah
> claims that this path, one we can come to know through
> contemplative practice and whose truth is validated by
> inner experience, is the cosmic path, and that our experi-
> ence is only a recapitulation of God's own way into the
> world.

Kabbalah is more properly regarded as *theosophy*, a religious
doctrine or system grounded in mystical insights, not *theology*,
which is a rationalistic study of those same doctrines. The kabbalist, whether in medieval Spain or in the modern world, more
often than not is someone who has undergone a profound, life-
altering apprehension of the divine (a technical term for this is
*noesis)* and who seeks not just to understand it on an intellectual
level, but to repeat the experience again and again. The *Sefirot*
are an attempt to objectively describe something that almost by
definition resists description: the immanence, or concrete presence, of God.

In the mid–twelve hundreds, Asher ben David, Isaac the
Blind's nephew, compared the *Sefirot* to God's garments. If He
didn't wear them, ben David said, His light would be too blind-

ing for us to see Him at all. As we look first at one garment and then another, our eyes grow accustomed to the light, and we are able to see more and more of God Himself.

The *Sefirot* begin and end in boundlessness: *Ein Sof,* "the infinite" or "without end." *Ein Sof* is the highest, most absolute level of the divine. It is indivisible, indescribable. In the words of the *Zohar:*

> Ein Sof *does not abide being known,*
> *does not produce end or beginning.*
> *Primordial Nothingness brought forth beginning and end.*

*Ein Sof* is monotheism brought to an extreme. It is the original, unmediated essence of God, so self-contained, so indivisible, so eternal and unchanging that you can only say what it is not, rather than what it is. But if you add a zero to a one, as Arthur Green observes (one of the few *Gematria* that makes sense in English), you create a ten—not ten separate, exclusive entities, but ten aspects of the indivisible One that are already existent within it. And this ten is the *Sefirot.*

## CHARACTERISTICS OF THE *SEFIROT*

### I. *Keter*

*Keter,* the first and highest of the *Sefirot,* literally means "crown." There are many traditions and mythologies that influence how the *Sefirot* are depicted. In Rabbi Luria's creation story, the universe was originally a huge man made out of *sefirot,* called Adam Kadmon. *Keter* was the top of his head. In other accounts, the *Sefirot* are arranged in a circle; *Keter* is its first and last point—twelve o'clock, as it were. When the *Sefirot* are depicted as an upside-down tree rooted in heaven, *Keter* is the cosmic "root of roots" (see diagrams). The first glimmering of desire, the first urge toward movement and multiplicity, *Keter* is known by the divine name *Ehyeh,* which means "I shall be." It is also called *Ayin,* or Nothingness. Various esoteric traditions assign the *Sefirot* physical characteristics, such as color and location in space; some *Sefirot* are particularly associated with Hebrew letters. *Keter*'s letter is *aleph,* the first letter of the Hebrew alphabet; its direction is east, toward the rising sun.

## 2. *Hokhmah*

From *Keter* comes *Hokhmah,* or Wisdom. If *Keter* is undifferentiated nothingness, *Hokhmah* is an infinitesimal point that contains within it all that will ever be. *Hokhmah* is the universe before the Big Bang, except that it never explodes (the *Sefirot* are not a sequence of events in time—each of them exists simultaneously and eternally). *Hokhmah* contains the potential for all of the truth and wisdom that will be manifested in creation. It is said that when God needed to create laws to rule the universe, he studied Torah. *Hokhmah* is the Torah that existed before the revelation at Sinai, before even words and letters came to be. Its letter is *yod,* the smallest in the Hebrew alphabet, and the first letter of the tetragrammaton. (The tetragrammaton is the four-letter name of God [YHWH]. Pious Jews do not pronounce it out loud, instead they say *"adonai,"* which means "the Lord.")

### 3. *Binah*

*Binah*, Contemplation or Understanding, is *Hokhmah's* mate. She is the womb that receives the divine seed of *Hokhmah* and gives birth to the seven lower *Sefirot*. *Binah* is sometimes particularly referred to as the mother of the tenth *Sefirah*, *Shekhinah*, with whom she shares many characteristics. *Hokhmah* and *Binah* are inseparable—*Hokhmah* lights up *Binah's* palace, making it visible; *Binah*, in turn, reflects *Hokhmah's* light, which would otherwise be too concentrated to be seen. *Binah's* letter is *heh*, the second and fourth letters of the tetragrammaton. Among the many ideas and images associated with *Binah* are palace, womb, and repentance.

From *Keter*, the merest stirring within the supernal stillness of the infinite *Ein Sof*, emerges *Hokhmah*, the spark or seed of existence, and *Binah*, the womb, the deepest font of being, in which it germinates. Their children, the seven "lower" *Sefirot*, are the attributes of the God we pray to, and in whose image we are made. Each of these seven so-called lower *Sefirot* has its counterpart in our own souls.

### 4 and 5. *Hesed and Gevurah*

*Hesed* means "love," "grace," or "compassion"; it is God's overflowing benevolence and generosity—His mercy and kindness. The right hand of the primal Adam, *Hesed* is associated with the south and with the biblical patriarch Abraham.

*Hesed's* opposite (really its complement) is *Gevurah* or *Din*, which means "judgment," "might," or "power." As every parent quickly learns, love alone will not suffice to raise independent, responsible children. A parent has to set boundaries, to be disciplined and strong as well or the children will not mature—

they won't even know that they are loved. *Gevurah* is the left hand of the primal Adam; the biblical figure it is most associated with is Isaac, and its direction is north. As Isaac's father, Abraham, dedicated himself to God with unstinting love *(Hesed)*, ready even to sacrifice his child, so Isaac, bound to the altar, tremblingly beheld God's fearsomeness *(Gevurah)*. From *Hesed* comes the passion that inspires saints, from *Gevurah* the awe of God's terrible majesty. One without the other is a recipe for disaster: *Hesed* unbound can lead to zealotry or cringing obedience; *Gevurah* to cruelty and tyranny. *Gevurah* and *Hesed* must constantly balance each other. Evil comes into the world through the left side, the side of *Gevurah*, from an excess of harsh judgment. If too much love stifles, too much discipline destroys.

## 6. *Tif'eret*

When *Hesed* and *Gevurah* are precisely balanced, we have *Tif'eret*. The perfect union of love and power, mercy and judgment, *Tif'eret* means "glory," or "beauty." Another name for *Tif'eret* is "the Holy One, blessed be he," the rabbinic name for God. More than any of the other *Sefirot*, *Tif'eret* is the aspect of God we worship and emulate; *Tif'eret* is also called *Rahamim* (compassion) or *Emet* (truth); it unites the other nine *Sefirot*. Arthur Green observes that the three Hebrew letters of *Emet* are the first, middle, and last letters of the alphabet, so "truth is stretched forth across the whole of Being, joining the extremes of right and left, *hesed* and *gevurah*, into a single integrated personality." *Tif'eret* is the spine of Rabbi Luria's primordial Adam and the trunk of the "tree of life"; the Bible character it is most associated with is Jacob, or Israel. *Tif'eret's* direction is east; it is also associated with humility, harmony, and the tenth *Sefirah,* the *Shekhinah* (with whom it seeks to be united; together they give birth to the human soul). Its letter is *vav,* the third letter of the tetragrammaton.

### 7 and 8. *Netzah and Hod*

*Netzah* and *Hod* are earthly counterparts to *Hesed* and *Gevurah. Netzah* means "triumph" or "eternity." It is the right leg of the primordial Adam; the biblical figure it is associated with is Moses. *Netzah* represents prophecy and God's active grace in the world; it is where the urge to "repair the world" comes from, the desire to right wrongs and institute better social systems. *Netzah* is also the source of the messianic urge, which can lead to grandiosity and zealotry. The overidentification of one's own will with God's, the conviction that nothing and no one should be allowed to stand in one's way when one's cause is just, has ironically been the direct cause of much grief and injustice.

If *Netzah* is the restless questing after transcendence, its complement, *Hod,* which means "majesty" or "beauty," is the wisdom that pays obeisance to mystery, gratefully accepting its own limitations, understanding that there are some things in life that cannot be changed or challenged. *Hod* is the left leg of the primordial Adam; the biblical character it is most associated with is Moses' brother Aaron, the priest, who was charged with maintaining the forms of worship. If Moses boldly acted in God's name at a historical moment, Aaron prostrated himself before Him and saw to it that He would receive proper deference for the rest of time.

### 9. *Yesod*

The synthesis of *Netzah* and *Hod* is *Yesod*, which means "foundation." Just as *Tif'eret* is the synthesis of *Hesed* and *Gevurah*, *Yesod* is the reconciliation of the opposite extremes of *Netzah* and *Hod*. *Yesod* is frequently called *Tzaddik*, or "the righteous one" (as in Proverbs 10:25—"When the storm passes the wicked man is gone/But the righteous is an everlasting foundation"). The *Tzaddik*'s mature faith is a stable compound of wisdom and zeal.

*Yesod* is the circumcised phallus of the primal Adam, the conduit through which the divine, fructifying forces of the *Sefirot* pass into the *Shekhinah* and thence to man. The biblical character associated with *Yesod* is Joseph; *Yesod* is also associated with peace, the covenant, the Tree of Life, and with redemption, remembrance, and the restoration of balance.

### 10. *Shekhinah* (or *Malkhut*)

The tenth *Sefirah* is *Shekhinah*, which means "that which dwells," referring to the tabernacle of God. The *Shekhinah* is the female vessel into which God pours his generative energies. It is through her that the One is made manifest in our plural world. When we feel the presence of God—when we intuit that we are walking on holy ground, when we feel "intimations of immortality," when we quake in the face of the *mysterium tremendum*, a Latin term that Christian mystics use to denote "overwhelming mystery"—we are feeling her. *Shekhinah* is also called *Malkhut*, or "the Kingdom," the place where the King presides in perfect peace and harmony and fulfillment. *Shekhinah* is the daughter of *Binah* and the bride of *Tif'eret*, she receives the emanations from above and gives birth to life below.

When humans perform *mitzvot*, when they fulfill the biblical laws and perform good deeds, it stimulates her desire for *Keter*; his spirit flows into her, and our spirits flow up through her.

According to the *Zohar*, the *Shekhinah* is the personification of the spirit of the Jewish people. She shares in their exile: when the Jewish people are restored to Israel, she will be restored to God. If the *Sefirot* are frequently compared to a tree or a fountain or a ladder, they are also a human body, a conduit of sexual energies: *Keter* pours his essence into the *Shekhinah*. *Shekhinah* is the mouth of the primal Adam; she is associated with King David and the matriarch Rachel. Her letter of the tetragrammaton is *he*. She is associated with the Sabbath (her erotic union with *Tif'eret* is echoed by the human lovemaking that observant Jews encourage on the Sabbath, a day that unites the divine and earthly realms), with the earth, the moon (a passive—that is, feminine—recipient of light), and with the rose. She is the object of the erotic poetry in the biblical Song of Songs, she is the Queen and the Rainbow and the Ark of the Covenant, the daughter and the matron and the Talmud. She is the End of Thought. If *Keter* is the upper crown, she is the lower; when the *Sefirot* are represented as a circle rather than as ramifications of the Tree of Life, she is the "last circle"—she appears to the left of *Keter* at approximately eleven o'clock (see diagram).

From *Keter*, down through the antitheses of excessive justice and excessive mercy, excessive zeal and excessive passivity, we arrive in the world of love and desire. The "right" *Sefirot* (*Hokhmah*, *Hesed*, and *Netzah)* are "masculine" and merciful; the left *Sefirot* (*Binah*, *Gevurah*, and *Hod)* are "feminine" and just and powerful. As we have seen, justice unsoftened by

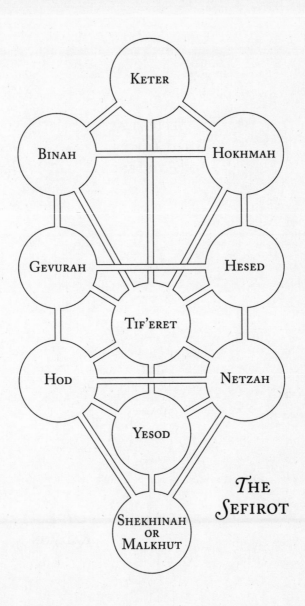

KETER

BINAH  HOKHMAH

GEVURAH  HESED

TIF'ERET

HOD  NETZAH

YESOD

SHEKHINAH
OR
MALKHUT

THE
SEFIROT

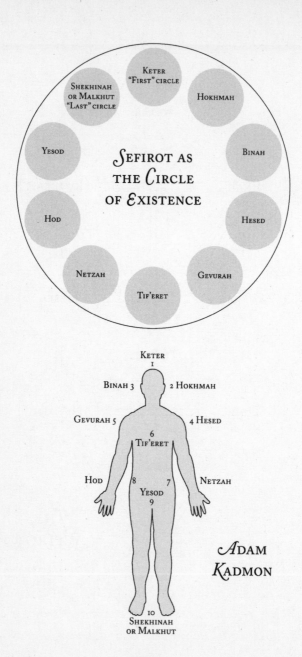

SEFIROT AS THE CIRCLE OF EXISTENCE

KETER "FIRST" CIRCLE

HOKHMAH

SHEKHINAH or MALKHUT "LAST" CIRCLE

BINAH

YESOD

HESED

HOD

NETZAH

GEVURAH

TIF'ERET

KETER
1

BINAH 3

2 HOKHMAH

GEVURAH 5

4 HESED

6
TIF'ERET

HOD

8

7

NETZAH

YESOD
9

ADAM KADMON

10
SHEKHINAH or MALKHUT

mercy leads to evil. The *Sefirot* of the "middle column" *(Keter,
Tif'eret, Yesod,* and *Shekhinah)* strike an ideal balance between
righteousness and compassion. Whether we envision them as
the fruits of a tree of life, as the rails of Jacob's ladder, as a primal man with a mind, heart, and phallus, or as a perfect circle—a model of eternity—the *Sefirot* are most of all, as Arthur
Green so eloquently expresses it, "a way of thinking for us, not
a body of knowledge. They are the choreography for a dance of
the mind, to be apprehended always by the left side of the
brain, that which appreciates poetry and hears its inner music."

## THE FOUR WORLDS: STAGES OF
## SPIRITUAL ASCENT

*All who are linked to My name,*
*Whom I have created,*
*Formed and made for My glory.*
—ISAIAH 43:7

The *Sefirot* provide a framework for conceptualizing the flow of
energy from one world, or level of being, into another; they are
also a vehicle for transcendence. They are a map of the spirit
and a guided meditation through the attributes of God. But to
the kabbalist, the universe contains more than just heaven and
earth: there are four worlds at the very least. The names of these
four worlds are taken from the verse in Isaiah cited above (the
first is translated as "linked"; the other three are synonyms for

"creation": "created," "formed," and "made"). Each world is successively closer to God.

Proceeding from the lowest to the highest, *Asiyah* is the world of doing; *Yetsirah* is the world of formation; *Beri'ah* is the world of creation; and *Atsilut*, the highest realm, is identified with God Himself ("linked to My Name"), where His presence is absolute and can only be experienced through ecstatic union—this world is the source of emanations or "flowing." Each of the three lower worlds contains *Sefirot* of their own; the *Sefirot* of each world are linked to those of another, forming an interdimensional daisy chain. Some kabbalists complicate this scheme even more, describing how each individual set of *Sefirot* in each individual world contains still another set of ten *Sefirot* (each existing in four or more dimensions). The potential combinations are as dizzying as anything you might find in the study of the human genome or the outer reaches of string theory. Although the kabbalists took the literal existence of these multiple worlds as seriously as today's physicists do the quantum realms, Arthur Green suggests that these multiple worlds are best understood as metaphors for the stages of an individual's spiritual development.

*Asiyah*, the world of "making" and "doing," is the world we live in day to day—the place where we are born and die, get and spend, endure wars and famines, and experience the joys of physical love and reproduction. The inhabitant of *Asiyah* relates to God as a subject does to his or her king, with fear and awe.

In *Yetsirah*, the next world, we relate to God as a child does to his or her father—as the Being who engendered us. The Divine Father is an authoritative, not to mention awesome figure; He may be exasperated with us, we may frequently disappoint Him, but we know that He ultimately loves and accepts us: He made us in His image, we are the flesh of His flesh. The symbol of *Yetsirah* is the angel, who serves God with total, loving devotion.

*Asiyah* and *Yetsirah* correspond to *yir'ah* and *ahavah*, the fear and love of God. They are reflected in the *Avinu Malkenu* ("Our Father, Our King") of the Yom Kippur liturgy and represent, as Arthur Green observes, the emotion that is required for the conduct of a conventional, nonmystical devotional life. The mystic, however, hungers for a closer, more intimate relationship with God, in which the boundaries between the human and the divine are dissolved.

So the third world is *Beri'ah*. In this world God is no longer the parent but the lover. The key biblical correlative for this relationship (it is a key text for much of the Kabbalah—the *Zohar* is filled with references to it) is the unabashedly erotic Song of Songs. Here is a particularly telling quotation from the *Zohar:*

> *Human beings are so confused in their minds.*
> *They do not see the way of truth in Torah.*
> *She calls out to them every day, in love,*
> *but they do not want to turn their heads.*
> *She removes a word from her sheath,*
> *is seen for a moment, then quickly hides away,*
> *but she does so only for those who know her intimately.*
>
> *A parable.*
> *To what can this be compared?*
> *To a beloved, ravishing maiden, hidden deep within her palace.*
> *She has one lover, unknown to anyone, hidden too.*

*Out of love for her, this lover passes by her gate constantly,*
*lifting his eyes to every side.*
*Knowing that her lover hovers about her gate constantly,*
*what does she do?*
*She opens a little window in her hidden palace,*
*revealing her face to her lover,*
*then swiftly withdraws, concealing herself.*
*No one near him sees or reflects, only the lover,*
*and his heart and his soul and everything within him*
*flow out to her.*
*He knows that out of love for him*
*she revealed herself for that one moment*
*to awaken love in him.*

The ultimate object of mystical experience is union, the total dissolution of the self into the object of devotion. In *Atsilut*, the fourth and final world, there is no king or father, neither I nor thou, lover nor beloved—we are "linked to the name," dissolved into the transcendent stillness, the unchangeable, absolute Oneness from which the *Sefirot* emanate and in which they eternally reside. As Arthur Green writes in *Ehyeh*, "God knows us in *Atsilut* as God's own self; the Knower, the knowledge, and the known are entirely one, indistinguishable from one another."

In a famous passage in *The Guide For the Perplexed*, Moses Maimonides described revelation as akin to a lightning flash that reveals a vast landscape to an observer, but only for an instant. The rest of religious life, he said, is an effort to recollect and comprehend what was so vividly but fleetingly glimpsed. So it is with the mystic. If you are lucky enough to have experienced that sense of divine union in a precious moment of grace, then the rest of your days will be dedicated to recapturing it, or at least to making sense of it. The esoteric tools of Kabbalah are designed to either deliberately induce the experience (as in Abulafia's "Path of Names") or, as with the *Sefirot* and the endlessly inventive decodings of Hebrew letters and biblical texts, to unlock and systematize its secrets.

## THE *ZOHAR:* THE HEART OF KABBALAH

Both of these impulses were fully expressed in the *Zohar*, or *The Book of Splendor*. An immense (it runs to at least five volumes) compilation of *Midrash* (biblical commentary), sermons, homilies, visionary passages, and dialogues and treatises on creation, emanation, the *Sefirot*, and the four worlds, the *Zohar* was ostensibly written in Aramaic by Rabbi Shimon bar Yochai and his circle, who lived in Palestine in the second century C.E.

A disciple of the great Talmudist Rabbi Akiva (the sole survivor, you might recall, of the fateful visit to the "orchard"), Shimon bar Yochai was a legendary figure, not only a saint and a scholar, but a heroic Jewish nationalist who resisted the Roman occupation of the Holy Land. The Talmud relates a story in which a fellow rabbi, Judah ben Guerim, complimented the Romans' engineering prowess in bar Yochai's presence, singling out their baths, steps, and roads. Shimon bar Yochai is said to have replied, "They build steps to put whores on them, baths to cultivate their bodies, and bridges to force us to pay tolls." When Rabbi Guerim reported him to the authorities as a sub-

versive, Shimon and his son Eleazar fled into the desert with
nothing but a jug of water and a bag of carobs to sustain them.
Eventually they took shelter in a cave. One of the carobs fell
into a cleft in a rock and a tree miraculously sprouted. Soon its
roots split open the rock, revealing a spring of fresh water. Legend has it that Shimon and his son remained in the cave for
thirteen years, studying Torah and composing the *Zohar*. It was
said that they buried themselves up to their necks in sand during the day to stay cool, only donning their clothes when they
prayed. The prophet Elijah himself summoned them from the
cave when the danger had passed.

The *Zohar* gives us lengthy exegeses of Torah, followed by
parables in which a donkey driver or a mysterious wise child
enlightens an assemblage of astonished rabbis; the notion of
Adam Kadmon, the primal Adam (a cosmic being composed of
*Sefirot* who preceded the biblical Adam), is developed at
length. Daniel C. Matt, the leading contemporary translator
and interpreter of the *Zohar*, describes it as "a mystical novel [in
which] Rabbi Shimon and the *havrayya* [companions] wander
through Galilee exchanging kabbalistic insights. . . . the plot of
the *Zohar* focuses ultimately on the *Sefirot*. By penetrating the
literal surface of the Torah, the mystical commentators trans-
form the biblical narrative into a biography of God."

Like the other seminal texts of Kabbalah, the origins of the
*Zohar* are murky. Starting in the 1280s, the well-regarded
Spanish kabbalist Moses ben Shem Tov de Leon, better known
today as Moses de Leon, began circulating manuscripts that he
claimed to have copied from an ancient, previously unknown
text by bar Yochai. How had de Leon obtained this treasure? In

one account, the great philosopher Nachmanides discovered the manuscript in Palestine, where he had settled after he was exiled from Spain. He sent it to his son in Catalonia, but the ship that was carrying it was diverted to Avila, where de Leon lived. Somehow it came into his possession. In another account, the manuscript was discovered in a vault by an Arab king. He sent it to Toledo to have it translated; from Toledo it found its way by unspecified means to Avila and de Leon. In still another telling, an Arab fishmonger found the scrolls in a cave and used them to wrap up his wares; one evening a kabbalist in the city of Safed in Palestine bought some fish from him and made the astonishing discovery as he was preparing his supper. Somehow the manuscript then traveled from Safed to Spain and de Leon. In yet another version, conquistadores came upon it at an academy in Heidelberg and brought it back to Spain.

There are undoubtedly other stories too, but the fact is that nobody knows how—or for that matter, *if*—de Leon acquired the manuscript, or more to the point, whether such a manuscript ever existed. In 1305 a young rabbi named Samuel of Acre traveled to Spain to study Kabbalah. He arrived in Avila shortly after de Leon had died; there he was told (by someone who heard it from someone who heard it from someone else) that when a rich citizen named Joseph de Avila had offered to marry his son to de Leon's daughter in exchange for the original manuscript of the *Zohar*, de Leon's widow had confessed to him that there was no "original" to be had—all of the *Zohar* had come out of her husband's head. When asked why he hadn't claimed authorship (after all, de Leon was a prolific and greatly respected writer in his own right), she told him that her husband had cynically declared, "If I told people that I am the author, they would pay no attention nor spend a farthing on the book, for they would say that these are but the workings of my own imagination. But now that they hear that I am copying from the book *Zohar* which Simeon ben Yohai wrote under the inspiration of the Holy Spirit, they are paying a high price for it as you know."

Samuel of Acre himself took this story with a grain of salt, but Heinrich Graetz, the renowned nineteenth-century historian, found in it confirmation of his own generally low opinion of mystics. In his classic history of Judaism he characterized de Leon as the basest of charlatans and the *Zohar* as a shameless fraud.

The consensus among scholars today is that de Leon probably did write a great deal (but almost certainly not all) of the *Zohar.* But whether it was discovered, compiled, edited, or invented, it is undoubtedly one of the world's greatest spiritual documents. Within a few centuries of its appearance the *Zohar* had become the most important book in the canon of Jewish religious texts after the *Tanakh* and the Talmud. "I thank God every day that I was not born before the *Zohar* was revealed," Rabbi Pinkhas of Koretz would declare in the eighteenth century. "For it was the *Zohar* that sustained me in my faith as a Jew."

## SAFED, PALESTINE, AND RABBI ISAAC LURIA
## ("THE ARI")

In the centuries following the appearance of the *Zohar* in 1280, the Kabbalah spread into Italy and the East from Spain. Some of its more important expositors were Bahya ben Asher from Saragossa, whose commentary on the Torah would be the first kabbalistic book to be printed in its entirety, in 1492, and Hayyim ben Samuel of Lerida, who offered a kabbalistic exposition of *Halakha* (Jewish law) called *Zeror ha-Hayyim*. Joseph ben Shalom wrote on the transmigration of souls and essayed a kabbalistic interpretation of Aristotle. Some kabbalists, like Shem Tov ben Shem Tov (1400–1480), made the radical declaration that Judaism made no sense at all unless it was interpreted from a kabbalistic point of view. Slowly but surely, Kabbalah was penetrating into the mainstream.

If the thirteen hundreds and the fourteen hundreds were a time of consolidation and synthesis for the Kabbalah, they were a dreadful epoch for the Jews of Europe and especially of the Iberian Peninsula. The Black Death swept through Europe in the thirteen hundreds, not only killing thousands of Jews but bringing many reprisals against its survivors, who were accused of deliberately spreading the disease. In Spain, the so-called golden age of Jewish, Christian, and Muslim cooperation was fast becoming a memory, as Christians slowly but surely forced the Moors out of the Iberian Peninsula in what became known as the *Reconquista*. The persecutions and forced conversions that had begun in the late twelve hundreds finally culminated in 1492 when hundreds of thousands of Jews—some of whose ties to Spain went back more than a millennium—were expelled.

Rational, philosophical Judaism was seemingly impotent to protect the Jews from their persecutors; Kabbalah, in contrast, held out hope for immediate redemption. Staggered by this unending series of crises, Jewish mystics increasingly looked forward to an imminent apocalypse and the advent of the Messiah. "The decree from above that one should not discuss kabbalistic teaching in public was meant to last only for a limited time—until 1490," declared one anonymous kabbalist. "We then entered the period called 'the last generation,' and then the decree was rescinded, and permission given. . . . And from 1540 onward the most important *mitzvah* will be for all to study it in public, both old and young, since this, and nothing else, will bring about the coming of the Messiah."

An anonymous but widely distributed book called *Kaf ha-Ketoreth* reinterpreted the Book of Psalms as a prophecy of End Times. A mysterious man, possibly from Ethiopia or Yemen, calling himself David the Reubenite, met with the Pope in the 1520s, seeking his help to raise an army to take back the Holy Land. Inspired by the Reubenite, Dogo Pires, a Marrano (a converted Jew) in Lisbon, took on the name Solomon Molcho and declared himself the Messiah. The Reubenite would finish his life in a Spanish prison; Molcho would be burned at the stake. Still the Jews awaited their redeemer.

By the middle of the sixteenth century, the center of Jewish mystical life had moved to Palestine, where the comparatively tolerant Ottomans ruled, especially to the city of Safed in the Galilee. Many of the leading lights of the Jewish intellectual world lived there and knew each other, including Elijah de Vidas (1518–1592), the author of *Reshit Hokhma* (The Beginning of Wisdom); Moses Cordovero (1522–1570), one of Kabbalah's greatest thinkers and the author of *Pardes Rimmonim* (The Garden of Pomegranates); Eleazar Azikri (1533–1600), author of the *Sefer Haredim* (The Book of the Pious); Solomon ben Moses Alkabetz (1505–?), who wrote the Sabbath hymn *"Lekha Dodi"* (Come, My Beloved); Hayyim Vital (1542–1620), author of the *Etz Hayyim* (The Tree of Life); and the legal authority (and mystic) Joseph Caro (1488–1575), author of the *Shulḥan Arukh* (The Set Table), an encyclopedic guide to Jewish observance that is still referred to today. Rabbi Lawrence Kushner has facetiously compared this small medieval textile center to the Upper West Side of Manhattan.

Most influential of all was Isaac Luria Ashkenazi, "the Ari" (the acronym for his name spells out the Hebrew word for lion). Rabbi Luria was born in Jerusalem in 1534 but grew up in Egypt. He married his cousin at age fifteen and spent some years living in seclusion on the island Jazïrat al-Rawda on the Nile, studying Kabbalah. He was only thirty-five years old when he moved to Safed (possibly to study with Moses Cordovero, who died shortly after his arrival); he would die himself in an epidemic less than three years later, in 1572. Although a few of his poems and hymns are widely known, he never wrote a book. "I can hardly open my mouth to speak without feeling as though the sea burst its dams and overflowed," he is said to have declared, in a beautifully eloquent testimony to the mystic's sense of repleteness. "How then shall I express what my soul has received, and how can I put it in a book?"

The little we know about Luria's life is overlaid with legend—for example, that he had memorized entire volumes of the Talmud by the time he turned eight; that he ascended with angels to heavenly academies to study Torah with rabbis Shimon bar Yochai, Akiva, and Eleazar; and that Elijah himself (with whom he had had frequent conversations since early childhood) instructed him to move to Safed. In his disciple Hayyim Vital's often-quoted words:

> The Ari overflowed with Torah. He was thoroughly expert in Scripture, *Mishnah, Talmud, Pilpul, Midrash, Agadah, Ma'aseh Bereshit and Ma'aseh Merkavah*. He was expert in the language of trees, the language of birds, and the speech of angels. He could read faces in the manner outlined in the *Zohar* [see page 75]. He could discern all that any individual had done, and could see what they would do in the future. He could read people's thoughts, often before the thought even entered their mind. He knew future events, was aware of everything happening here on earth, and what was decreed in heaven.

Luria only accepted a few students and he would teach them while taking long walks around the vicinity of Safed, where he discovered by intuition the burial places of spiritual luminaries; he would commune with them by lying facedown on their graves. Most of what we know about Luria and his teachings comes through the writings of Hayyim Vital and, less authoritatively, Israel Sarug, who introduced Lurianic kabbalism to Italy, from whence it spread across Europe.

Many of Luria's teachings are well-nigh incomprehensible. In Rabbi Lawrence Kushner's words, "You don't 'get into' Lurianic Kabbalah; you struggle to make sense of it." But Luria's most important contribution to Kabbalah is relatively easy to understand—his myth of creation.

─────────────── How Come? ───────────────

*If kabbalists detected past lives from the lines on a person's face,
could they read palms too?*

Palm reading, or *chiromancy,* dates back at least to Hellenic times
in the Near East. From the very beginning there were opposing
systems: one was intuitive, and depended upon the psychic gifts
of the interpreter, the other was linked to astrology and was objective and systematic. Chiromancy entered Judaism during the
*Merkabah* period, in the second century C.E. One influential manuscript was called *Re'iyyat ha-Yadayim le-Ehad me-Hakhmei Hodu,*
or "Reading the Hands by an Indian Sage." The *Zohar* includes
extensive passages dealing with palm and forehead reading.

## THE LURIANIC COSMOLOGY:
### *TZIMTZUM, SHEVIRAH,* AND *TIKKUN OLAM*

The world came into being, Rabbi Luria taught, when God
withdrew a portion of Himself from Himself (*tzimtzum,* or
contraction) to make room for creation. Into this empty space,
God projected a stream of light, which formed itself into the
primal Adam (Adam Kadmon). Light came out of the primal
Adam's eyes, nose, and mouth and took the shapes of the ten *Sefirot.* But those vessels weren't strong enough to contain the divine essence—the highest vessels cracked and the lowest seven
shattered, dividing the empty space into two realms, an upper
and a lower world. The world we live in today is a product of
this shattering *(shevirah);* what we know as God's creation is
really a mixture of *kelipot*—shards of the lower *Sefirot*—and
remnant sparks of God's divine light. The sparks long to be re-
united with their source, but the *kelipot* won't let them go, for

the admixture of divine light and corrupt matter is the source of evil. This is why people were created—to fix the world *(tikkun olam)*, to liberate the sparks.

The Adam who lived in the Garden of Eden (a different Adam than Adam Kadmon) was meant to be the only person ever created—he carried within him all the souls of mankind. If he hadn't fallen, the universe would have been returned to perfection long ago, but when he did, the shattering that created our world was recapitulated on the human level—each of Adam's innumerable souls was scattered to do the job that Adam should have completed himself. These souls are continually reincarnated until they have fulfilled their task. If they are Gentiles, they need to follow their own prescriptions for righteousness; if they are Jews, they must follow *Halakha*. Every time a Jew performs a *mitzvah*—every time one of the 613 commandments is obeyed—a spark is liberated, diminishing the power of evil in the world. When the last spark is raised, evil will be utterly extirpated, clearing the way for the Messiah to arrive. According to Luria, this is the deeper reason for the Diaspora—the Jews had to be scattered among all the nations so they could lift sparks throughout the entire world. When the Messiah comes, all of the scattered souls will resume their place within Adam and the whole world will literally be as one.

Three separate strains merge in Rabbi Luria's version of Kabbalah: the halakhic obedience of traditional Judaism, the intense pietism and penitence of the *Hasidei Ashkenaz* (the penitence is for personal sin, original sin, and for the sins committed in past incarnations), and the Sefirotic system of the *Zohar*. At a moment in history when the Jewish people seemed to be at their lowest ebb, the Lurianic Kabbalah offered an appealing explanation: Far from powerless, the scattered members of the nation of Israel were the key soldiers in a cosmic campaign to bring a manifestly flawed universe back into conformity with its original plan—they were virtually collaborators on the recreation of the world. If their covenant with God required them to live up to high ideals, they, in turn, were working to assure that the Deity would live up to His!

# A Would-Be Messiah,
# the Baal Shem Tov,
# and the Twentieth Century

*Behold, a son will be born to Mordecai Zevi in the year 5386 [1626] and he will be called Shabbatai Zevi. He will subdue the great dragon, and take away the strength of the piercing serpent and the strength of the crooked serpent, and he will be the true messiah.*

—FROM A PROPHETIC VISION BY NATHAN OF GAZA

### THE MYTH OF JOSEPH DELLA REINA:
### WHY THE MESSIAH STILL HASN'T COME

A few years before the Jews were expelled from Spain in 1492, a Spanish kabbalist named Joseph della Reina was said to have broken into a Roman Catholic church, accompanied by several of his disciples. There he attempted, by use of divine names, incantations, and other sorceries, to capture the demon Samael and compel him to use his powers to protect the Jews. The rabbi overpowered the evil spirit at first, but he was defeated by his own compassion. Though he refused to give the demon anything to eat, when Samael pleaded for just one whiff of church incense, the rabbi gave in. The incense turned out to be so potent that the demon's strength was instantly restored; he threw off his bonds and flew away.

Some scholars have interpreted this story as a critical parable about the so-called New Christians or *conversos* of Spain and Portugal—Jews who had avoided exile by converting to Christianity. Even if they secretly maintained some Jewish rituals, they profaned themselves by their public participation in Christian rites. The merest whiff of Christianity, it was suggested, was enough to destroy any hope they might have for redemption.

Rabbi della Reina is a genuine historic figure (he was the author of several messianic tracts), but his story didn't gain wide currency until many years after his death. In 1519, Rabbi Abraham be-Rabbi Eliezer ha-Levi wrote a version of the tale declaring that, as a result of della Reina's misadventure, the advent of the Messiah had been delayed by forty years—most of which time had passed already. Ironically, this dark parable was now offered as a harbinger of hope. Some decades later Rabbi Luria commented on the story, noting that Rabbi della Reina had been reincarnated as a black dog.

Shlomo Navarro, a kabbalist from Jerusalem, wrote the best-known version of the story around 1660. In this version, della Reina lives near Safed. He and five trusted disciples summon first Elijah, then the angels Sandalphon, Akhtariel, and Metatron, and demand their assistance. Although each angel warns della Reina that his efforts are doomed to failure, they nonetheless teach him what he needs to know: how to use the sacred names to cross impassable mountains, deserts and an ocean, breach Samael's remote fortress, and subdue the demon. Once

Samael and his wife, Lilith, are delivered into God's power, the celestial beings promise, then the Messiah, who himself is praying for their success, will be immediately dispatched to earth. The rabbi and his disciples do all that they are told—they recite the proper formulas and prayers, they purify themselves with punishing fasts and by bathing in the sea. When at last they corner the demons, who are disguised as black dogs, they vanquish them by placing lead plates engraved with the Holy Names on their heads. But once again, the rabbi is undone by his compassion. Fortified by a sniff of frankincense, the demons rally and defeat him. Navarro adds a coda to the story, in which della Reina "gave up all hope of the world to come and made a covenant with the malicious Lilith." The ex-rabbi, now an arch-sensualist, entertained himself by ordering demons to fetch him whatever (and whoever) struck his fancy—including the queen of Greece, whose favors he enjoyed while she slept. When della Reina learned that the cuckolded king of Greece had found him out and that he was about to be arrested, he threw himself into the sea and drowned. Though these stories sound quaint and fanciful today, a bit like fairy tales, they have an undeniable poignancy when they are read in their grim historical context.

Messianism had always been an element of mainstream Judaism and it was becoming an increasingly important aspect of Kabbalah, but in the aftermath of the expulsion, it took on a new urgency. Many kabbalists in Luria's day had settled on 1575 as the most likely year for the Messiah's advent. Luria's chief disciple, Rabbi Hayyim Vital, didn't know precisely *when* the Messiah would reveal himself, but he was quite certain that he knew who the Messiah was. Along with the monumental *Etz Hayyim* (Tree of Life) and *Sefer ha-Shearim* (Book of

Gates), Hayyim Vital left a diary, covering forty years, which was dedicated almost entirely to proving the proposition that he himself was the Messiah. He didn't declare himself because he was waiting for the work of *tikkun olam*—the repair of the world—to be done. When the last spark was gathered up, he would be ready.

Although Rabbi Hayyim Vital had done his best to keep the Lurianic Kabbalah within a small circle of believers, it quickly spread across the Ottoman empire and Europe. By the mid-seventeenth century Kabbalah was, in Gershom Scholem's words, "the last religious movement in Judaism the influence of which became preponderant among all sections of the Jewish people in every country of the Diaspora, without exception. It was the last movement in the history of rabbinic Judaism which gave expression to a world of religious reality common to the whole people."

## HOPE AND CATASTROPHE:
### THE FALSE MESSIAH SHABBETAI ZEVI

The seventeenth century brought new horrors to Jewry. Between 1618 and 1648, the Thirty Years' War had devastated Europe. Although its combatants were Catholics and Protestants, both sides had frequently turned on the Jews. Starting in 1648, the Cossack Bogdan Chmielnicki's revolt against the Polish rulers of Ukraine (and especially their Jewish allies) resulted in the displacement, forced conversion, rape, and murder of hundreds of thousands of Jews. The Russian–Swedish War of 1655 took a staggering toll on Eastern European Jewry as well.

Shabbetai Zevi (also spelled Tzvi or Sevi) claimed to have been born on the ninth of Av (*Tisha b'Av*, the date of the destruction of the Temple—the traditionally accepted birthday of the Messiah) in Smyrna (modern-day Izmir, Turkey) in 1626. His father, a successful trader, groomed him for the rabbinate. He was considered to be a bright, if not particularly inspired, rabbi, with a gentle, pleasant manner and a beautiful singing voice.

But in his early twenties, Zevi began to exhibit the symptoms of what today would be immediately diagnosed as a bipolar mood disorder—he would suffer long periods of lethargy and depression, followed by bursts of ecstatic "illumination." During his exuberant periods, he would commit outrageous, blasphemous acts—pronouncing the name of God out loud, standing under a *chuppah* (a wedding canopy) and marrying himself to a Torah, contracting and canceling marriages with two different women (in 1664 he finally married a Chmielnicki orphan of dubious reputation). All the while, he wandered ceaselessly, preaching Kabbalah—from Smyrna to Greece, from Constantinople to Jerusalem and Cairo.

In 1665 he journeyed to Gaza to see a renowned young kabbalist named Nathan, who he had heard was a "physician of the soul." Like Rabbi Luria, Nathan had the ability to discern people's past incarnations by reading the lines on their faces; this gift allowed him to prescribe the appropriate penances that their souls required. Zevi went to him seeking help; far from curing his illness, Nathan, who already knew of Zevi's reputation, and who had been having visions about him for the past several months, informed him that he was the Messiah. Although Zevi resisted the notion at first, it didn't take Nathan long to persuade him of his destiny.

Zevi announced himself in Gaza and then, accompanied by a crowd of followers, journeyed to Jerusalem, where he rode a horse around its walls seven times. Almost immediately, rumors began to spread throughout the Diaspora—that the ten lost tribes of Israel had returned and were marching under the command of a prophet, that they had already conquered Mecca and were on their way to Persia.

Then Nathan issued his prophecy: all but a few of the divine sparks had been liberated, he declared, the rest could only be gathered by the Messiah himself, Shabbetai Zevi. There was a little more than a year left to do penance, he said, before the time of tribulations would begin. Zevi traveled to Smyrna, where, after a few quiet months, he again began to behave bizarrely. When a rabbinic court was convened to decide whether or not to open proceedings against him, Zevi, accompanied by a crowd of followers, smashed down the doors of one of the synagogues whose rabbi opposed him and began to read from the Torah. After encouraging his followers to utter the ineffable name of God—the unpronounceable tetragrammaton—out loud, he made a speech in which he compared his rabbinical opponents to *tref* (unclean, according to kashruth, the Jewish dietary laws) animals. He sang an old Castilian love song and interpreted it kabbalistically. He promised to deliver women from the curse of Eve. Then he announced the date of redemption—June 18, 1666—and declared that he would soon seize the crown of the sultan and make him his slave.

In February of 1666, the sultan—who had been uncharacteristically tolerant of Zevi's provocations—finally had him arrested. He was assigned comfortable quarters in prison and allowed to receive visitors; in April he was transferred to the fortress of Gallipoli, where the sultan incarcerated his most dangerous political enemies. But if Zevi was safely under lock and key, an unprecedented hysteria was spreading like wildfire across Europe as Jews of all economic and educational levels followed Nathan's prescriptions for penitence, preparing for their departure to the Holy Land. Some of the most renowned rabbis of the day urged them on. Gershom Scholem (who wrote the definitive book on Shabbetai Zevi) recounts:

> Many people fasted for the whole week: those who could not manage this fasted for two or three consecutive days every week and women and children at least every Monday and Thursday. . . . At night people would lie down naked in the snow for half an hour and scourge themselves with thorns and nettles. Commerce came to a standstill everywhere. Many sold their houses and property to provide themselves with money for the journey to the Holy Land, while others made no such provisions, being convinced that they would be transported on clouds. . . . Poems in honor of Shabbetai Zevi and Nathan were composed in Yemen, Kurdistan, Constantinople, Salonika, Venice, Ancona, Amsterdam and many other places.

And then, on September 16, 1666—catastrophe. The sultan offered Zevi a choice between being put to death immediately or converting to Islam. To the shock and horror of the thousands of Jews who had vested all their hopes in him, he chose the latter. Zevi changed his name to Aziz Mehmed Effendi and accepted the title of *Kapici Bashi* (Keeper of the Palace Gates), for which he received a handsome royal pension of 150 piastres a day.

If most of Jewry felt like they'd woken up with a tremendous hangover, a few of Zevi's disciples followed him into apostasy. Some of them adopted the forms of Islamic worship without renouncing their Judaism—these were called the *Doenmeh,* a Turkish word for "turncoats" or "dissidents." Their sect survived into at least the early twentieth century; a recent book by John Freely called *The Lost Messiah* claims that it still exists today. Nathan retained his faith in Zevi until the bitter end, declaring that his conversion was a part of his divine mission—Islam had its share of sparks too, and only the Messiah could gather them. Zevi was just pretending to be a Muslim; at the last possible moment, he would reveal himself in all his glory. When Zevi died on Yom Kippur in 1676, Nathan declared that this too was a part of his plan. The Messiah had gone into "occultation" for some period of time, he said—he had been absorbed into the "supernal lights." But before he found out what the Messiah's next move would be, Nathan himself died, in 1680.

Zevi was neither the first nor the last Jew who would claim to be the Messiah. What accounts for his massive appeal? Scholem suggests that it was a fortuitous combination of circumstances. The ground in Europe had been fertilized with blood. Reeling from the recent pogroms in the Ukraine, the Jewish people were unusually receptive to a message of redemption. Christian millenarian movements had been focusing on the mid–sixteen hundreds as the likeliest time for the apocalypse; they took a keen interest in Zevi's claims as well. Most important, the widespread acceptance of Lurianic kabbalism had given Nathan and Zevi doctrinal credibility. Nathan's prophecies had been promulgated from the Holy Land, and like so many biblical prophecies before them, they called mainly for repentance (and who could argue with that?). Paradoxically, this most radical of movements (before his apostasy Zevi had been given to ending his prayers with the antinomian benediction "blessed art Thou Who hath permitted forbidden things") succeeded to the extent that it did because of its ostensible conservatism.

The Shabbetain heresy would cast its shadow over a number of important mystic thinkers over the next century—scholars still argue about whether or not Jonathan Eybeschuetz, a gifted eighteenth-century Talmud scholar and kabbalist who lived in Prague, was a secret follower of Zevi. Jacob Frank (né Yakov ben Judah Leib Frankovich, 1726–1791), the son of a Zevi disciple and a would-be Messiah himself, recapitulated Zevi's movement on a smaller scale when he and his disciples converted to Roman Catholicism.

But if rabbinic Judaism would be much more cautious about Messianic claims after the Shabbetain disaster, mysticism was already too deeply ingrained in Jewish practice and belief to be extirpated. Kabbalah had become, in Rabbi Adin Steinsaltz's oft-quoted phrase, "the official theology of the Jewish people." By the middle of the next century, another popular mystical movement would sweep across Eastern Europe.

## THE BAAL SHEM TOV:
## A NEW KIND OF HASIDISM

Israel ben Eliezer, better known as the Baal Shem Tov or the Master of the Divine Name (the *BeShT* for short), was born in the village of Okup in the Carpathian Mountains in western Ukraine in 1698. Orphaned at age five (his father's last words to him were reputed to be "fear nothing other than God"), he was raised, by all accounts haphazardly, as a ward of the community. He worked as a school aide and a synagogue shammes (custodian) until he married the sister of a renowned Talmudist. After seven years of solitary study, he began to make a name for himself as an itinerant healer, preacher, and miracle worker. The *baal shem*s who wandered through rural Eastern Europe in the eighteenth century were not dissimilar to the sorcerers of Talmudic times. They were practical kabbalists who used prayers, invocations, amulets, herbal concoctions, and of course the names of angels, demons, and God, to cure illnesses and exorcise demons. The Baal Shem Tov was different—not only was he extraordinarily pious; he was a genuine visionary. And he transformed his uniquely personal vision into a far-reaching popular movement.

In an apparently authentic letter to his brother-in-law, the Besht described a conversation he had with the Messiah while he was in an elevated state; this took place on Rosh Hashanah, 1746.

> I went up from level to level until I entered the Palace of Moshiach, where Moshiach studies with the *Tannaim* and *tzaddikim*, as well as the Seven Shepherds. There I found extremely great rejoicing, but I did not know the

cause of this delight. At first I thought that it might be due to my having passed away from the physical world, God forbid. Later they told me that I had not yet died, for they have great pleasure on high when I effect mystical unifications in the world below through their holy Torah. However, to this very day, the nature of their joy remains unknown to me.

I asked *Moshiach*, "When will you come, master?" And he replied, "By this you shall know: it will be a time when your teachings become publicized and revealed to the world, and your well-springs have overflowed to the outside. [It will be when] that which I have taught you—and that which you have perceived of your own efforts—become known, so that others, too, will be able to perform mystical unifications and ascents of the soul like you. Then all the evil *klippos* will be destroyed, and it will be a time of grace and salvation."

Starting in the 1730s, the Besht began to attract a circle of disciples. He taught them that God was present in all things and in all people; that one cleaved to God not just in study but in ecstatic prayer and meditation (*dvekut*). Sparks of God were present even in evil things—this did not mean that God was the font of evil, he explained, only that everything, no matter how polluted, could be redeemed. Unlike the medieval *Hasidei Ashkenaz,* the Besht was not obsessed with guilt and asceticism; these new Hasids lived in a world that was filled with God's spirit. As the Besht's grandson, Rabbi Nachman of Breslov, would say, "the main thing is that one must struggle with all one's strength to be joyous always."

The Hasidism practiced by the Besht and the other founding *tzaddikim* was Lurianic kabbalism minus its daunting theosophical apparatus. Prayers were said in the vernacular, liquor was drunk, and there was wild dancing. Hasidism cheerfully acknowledged its followers' erotic yearnings, bodily and spiritual alike, even while it held them to the highest ethical (and halakhic) standards. But unlike the esoteric Kabbalah of Provence or Gerona, Hasidism was a genuinely popular movement. It acknowledged that not everybody could aspire to be saints or visionaries or scholars, only a few could reach the highest levels of spiritual development—but for that reason, you had to be ready to vest your faith in someone who could. The *tzaddik* or rebbe thus assumed a position not unlike the Messiah's in Nathan of Gaza's formulation, as an intermediary between the divine and the human. As Hasidism matured as a movement, its rebbes took on more and more power, providing the last word to their communities, not only on religious issues, but on marital, financial, and legal matters as well. Eventually, the *tzaddik*s functioned as a kind of royalty, passing their power down to their children.

In the introduction to his influential *Tales of the Hasidim* the philosopher Martin Buber wrote that Hasidism

> [made] manifest the reflection of the divine, the sparks of God that glimmer in all beings and all things, and taught how to approach them, how to deal with them, how to "lift" and redeem them, and re-connect them with their original root. The doctrine of the . . . *Shekhinah* as the Divine Presence which resides in this world receives a new and intimate significance and applicability. If you di-

rect the undiminished power of your fervor to God's world-destiny, if you do what you must do at this moment—no matter what it may be!—with your whole strength and with *kavvanah*, with holy intent, you will bring about the union between God and *Shekhinah*, eternity and time. You need not be a scholar or a sage to accomplish this. All that is necessary is to have a soul united within itself and indivisibly directed to its divine goal. The world in which you live, just as it is and not otherwise, affords you that association with God, which will redeem you and whatever divine aspect of the world you have been entrusted with. And your own character, the very qualities which make you what you are, constitutes your special approach to God, your special potential use for Him. Do not be vexed at your delight in creatures and things! But do not let it shackle itself to creatures and things; through these, press on to God.

By the time Buber was writing, in the mid–twentieth century, the Hasids had become the least liberal of Jews, and in many ways, some of the most isolated from modern life. By promoting Hasidic ideals about the conduct of life and spirituality (while playing down or altogether eliding their less congenial attributes such as occultism, dogmatism, and the lamentable corruptibility of its dynastic *tzaddikim*, many of whom had become as venal and inbred as any secular aristocracy), Buber helped reacquaint modern Judaism with an important and sadly neglected part of its spiritual heritage.

This is not the place to delve into Hasidism's fierce arguments with traditional Judaism, except to note that within a few generations the Hasidim and their rabbinic adversaries, the *Mitnagdim* (Hebrew for "opponents"), had much less to fear from each other than they did their common enemies: the Enlightenment, assimilation, Reform Judaism, Marxism—and the increasingly murderous anti-Semitism that would climax in Hitler's *shoah*. Though European Kabbalah has remained a central feature of Hasidism to the present day (especially within the Chabad movement, where Schneur Zalman's late-eighteenth-century *Tanya* remains a seminal text; Rabbi Yitzhak Ginsburgh is an influential proponent of *Chassidut* Kabbalah today), by the mid–nineteenth century, Hasidism had moved to the fringes of Judaism.

Even as the non-Jewish, Hermetic Qabala gained renewed attention in the Victorian era as a component of the British occult society, The Order of the Golden Dawn, the Jewish Kabbalah was quietly returning to its esoteric roots. In the back rooms of synagogues in Eastern Europe, in scattered enclaves in Palestine, isolated groups of holy men resumed their visionary activities. "Even today . . . men who are thoroughly 'modern' in their thought may draw inspiration from contemplating what Jewish prayer can be in its sublimest form," Gershom Scholem wrote elegiacally in the 1940s of Beth-el, a kabbalistic center founded in the mid–seventeen hundreds in Jerusalem by a Yemenite rabbi named Shalom Sharabi. "Kabbalism becomes at the end of its way what it was at the beginning: a genuine esotericism, a kind of mystery-religion which tries to keep the *profanum vulgus* at arm's length."

THE TWENTIETH CENTURY:

JEWISH MYSTICISM REBORN

Although Palestine had been a refuge for kabbalists since the Middle Ages, in the first part of the twentieth century Rabbi Abraham Isaac Kook (1865–1935) and Rabbi Yehuda Ashlag (1886–1955) combined their esoteric studies with an active engagement in the modern world. Kook, who was descended from important *Mitnagdim* and Hasidim, was one of the few among the Orthodox rabbinate of his day to embrace Zionism, identifying the state of Israel as he did with the restoration of the *Shekhinah*. He made *aliyah* in 1904 (the literal meaning of *aliyah* is "ascent"; the word is used to describe leaving the congregation to read the Torah in a synagogue service or, in this case, a journey to the Holy Land) and became chief rabbi of the Orthodox Ashkenazic community in Palestine in 1921. Although Kook's tolerance of secularity caused no end of controversy among his flock, he was an impassioned mystic. "I love everybody," he would write. "It is impossible for me not to love all people, all nations. With all the depth of my being, I desire to see them grow toward beauty, toward perfection. My love for the Jewish people is with more ardor, more depth. But my inner desire reaches out with a mighty love toward all."

Ashlag emigrated from Poland to Palestine in the 1920s. Though ultra-Orthodox, he was also a socialist. Ashlag wrote vast commentaries on Lurianic kabbalism and the *Zohar* (which he also translated into Hebrew). His main disciples were Rabbi Yehuda Brandwein (1904–1969) and his two sons, Baruch Shalom and Shlomo Benyamin. Brandwein's son-in-law, Rabbi Avraham Sheinberger, founded a commune in Israel called *Or Ganuz* (The Hidden Light). Brandwein was the uncle of the first wife of Philip Berg, the founder of the Kabbalah Centre (Berg is now divorced from her and estranged from most of their eight children). Though Berg identifies Ashlag as the founder of the Kabbalah Centre, Ashlag and Brandwein's heirs vehemently deny any current association with him.

Professor Gershom Scholem (1897–1982) of Hebrew University, Jerusalem, delivered the lectures that formed the basis of *Major Trends in Jewish Mysticism* in New York City in 1938; the book's second edition appeared in 1948, the year that Israel became a nation. In the intervening decade, six million European Jews had been murdered. The worst of the killing had been in Poland, Ukraine, and Lithuania—the heartland of Hasidic and halakhic culture. A whole world, a whole way of life, had vanished.

Ironically, the Holocaust would play a significant role in bringing the Kabbalah back to life, as would Scholem himself, although he thought he was writing its eulogy. An assimilated German Jewish student of mathematics and philosophy, Scholem had switched to Oriental languages in the early 1920s, writing his doctoral dissertation on the *Sefer-ha-Bahir*. As librarian of Hebrew University from 1923 to 1927, he rescued hundreds of historic manuscripts on mysticism from archives in Berlin, Poland, and Lithuania that would have otherwise been destroyed by the Nazis. What's more, he read them, authenticated them, arranged them in a credible chronology, and did his best to make sense of them on their own terms.

Until Scholem, the scholarly world had paid scant attention to Kabbalah, regarding it as something of an embarrassment, "a silly hodge-podge of numerological and alphabetical abracadabra (see page 94), childish beliefs, incantations, and various other kinds of

mumbo jumbo," as Nathan Ausubel, a popular writer on Judaism, would memorably characterize it in the 1940s. Scholem
provided Jewish mysticism with a historical and intellectual
frame of reference that, for the first time, made it possible to
study it in a dispassionate way. A towering figure in academia, an
intellectual pioneer of formidable erudition, strong opinions, and
considerable eloquence, Scholem still dominates the study of
Jewish mysticism, two decades after his death. Recently Moshe
Idel, who teaches at Hebrew University, has challenged some of
Scholem's assertions, especially about the influence of Christian
Gnostics on Jewish mystics from the rabbinic era (Idel suggests
that the Jews more likely influenced the Christians, a contention
that archaeological evidence—especially the trove of Gnostic
scrolls uncovered at Nag Hammadi in 1945—seems to support).

If the assimilated Jews of Western Europe and America had

---

### How Come?

*What Does "Abracadabra" Have to Do with Kabbalah?*

Remember the story mentioned above about Rava's *golem,* cited
in the Babylonian Talmud? Aryeh Kaplan points out some interesting G*ematria* associated with the phrase "Rava created a man"
*(Rabha bara gabhra).* In Hebrew the second word is the first word
reversed, the third word is the same as the second, except a *gim-
mel* precedes it. Its numerical value is 612, one less than the number of bones and blood vessels in the human body. This suggests
that the man is slightly less than human (a man without a soul).
The phrase is quite similar to the familiar Hebrew phrase *abra
k'adabra* (translated, "I will create as I speak").

---

regarded the Hasidim with condescension or contempt before the Holocaust, in its immediate aftermath they would embrace them as a saving remnant from a lost world. Starting in the early 1950s, Rabbi Menachem Mendel Schneerson (1902–1994), who had studied mathematics in Berlin and engineering at the Sorbonne, assumed the leadership of the Chabad-Lubavitch movement, which had relocated to Brooklyn, New York. Largely as a result of his aggressive outreach, it became the fastest-growing denomination in Judaism, with centers in forty-five states and more than sixty countries, especially behind the former Iron Curtain, where it is deliberately reseeding Jewish culture today.

Because of the poetic mysticism that imbued his writings and his powerful commitment to social justice, Joshua Abraham Heschel (1907–1972), a refugee from Nazi Europe and a descendent of great first-generation Hasidic figures like Pinkhas of Koretz, Yitzhok of Berdichev, and Dov Baer, would have a strong influence on the generation of rabbis he trained at the Jewish Theological Seminary. Another refugee, Zalman Schachter-Shalomi, who arrived in the United States in 1940 as a teenager, would become a leader in the countercultural *havurah* (literally "circle" or "group of friends") and Jewish Renewal movements in the 1960s.

After the war, mainstream Judaism became much more attentive to Martin Buber's and Franz Rosenzweig's appreciations of Jewish mysticism; Yiddish writers like I. L. Peretz, Sholem Asch, Sholom Aleichem, and Chaim Grade enjoyed a new intellectual cachet when they were translated and anthologized by Irving Howe in the 1950s. S. Y. Agnon, who was

born in Galicia as Shmuel Yosef Czaczkes in 1888, would win
the Nobel Prize for Literature in 1966; I. B. Singer, the apos-
tate son of a Hasidic scholar and brother of the popular Yiddish writer I. J. Singer, would win the Nobel in 1978.

Among the political and cultural upheavals that roiled the
1960s was a restless questing for a more expressive, overt spirituality. Many Jews, not finding this in the synagogues they'd
grown up in, experimented with psychedelic drugs and Eastern
religions; some returned frustrated, looking instead for a mysticism that was rooted in their natal culture. The antiwar and
environmental movements, feminism, gay liberation, and other
expressions of the counterculture inspired some of these ac-
tivists to look for correlatives in Jewish culture.

Some of them—like *tikkun olam*—were there already, although unrecognized or ignored or denied by mainstream Judaism; some of them had to be created from scratch. As Jewish
women carved out a space for themselves in Jewish observance,
they recovered female characters from scripture (like Moses'
sister Miriam) and invented rituals, like *Rosh Khodesh*, the cel-
ebration of the new moon. For all of its overt eroticism, its
fetishization of the *Shekhinah*, its talk of balancing the female
and the male columns of the *Sefirot*, Kabbalah had always been
overwhelmingly masculine. Female writers like Sylvia Boor-
stein, Rabbi Tirzah Firestone, and Tamar Frankiel have started
to change that today (see page 97).

The *havurah* movement that began in the late 1960s, in which
small collectives of progressive Jews worshipped, studied, and, in
some cases, lived together, spawned dozens of influential books
by a new generation of Jewish intellectuals, including Michael
and Sharon Strassfeld, Arthur Green, Zalman Schachter-Sha-

---

### How Come?

*Catholics have their St. Teresa and Joan of Arc. Why weren't there any women kabbalists?*

How could there have been? Tradition had it that Kabbalah was forbidden to anyone who wasn't male, married, and expert in Torah, and halakhic Judaism forbade teaching women Torah (though it permitted them to teach it to themselves). But that doesn't answer the question. The fact is, there were. Born in 1815, Hannah Rachel of Ludmir, the Maiden of Ludmir, was the only daughter of a Hasidic shopkeeper named Monisch Werbermacher, who had vowed to raise his unborn child to become a sage. Hannah Rachel was a prodigy, learning vast amounts of Talmud by the time she was nine. She was said to have fallen in love with a Jewish soldier, but he was redeployed before they could wed. Shortly after this disappointment she became ill and fell into a trance; when she woke up she declared that she had been to heaven.

When her father died, she bought a small green hut near the marketplace and set herself up as a *tzaddik,* praying and studying while wearing phylacteries and tallith; she quickly gained repute as a wonder-worker. A rabbinic court eventually ordered her to cease her activities, certain that she was possessed by a demon; finally, they compelled her to marry. When she refused to consummate the marriage they excommunicated her. At age fifty-five, she found her way to Jerusalem, where, once again, she set herself up as a rebbe, wearing men's clothing and praying daily at the Wailing Wall until her death at age ninety. Though she was renowned as a saint and a sage, her burial place is unknown and her teachings were lost.

---

lomi, and Arthur Waskow. Waskow and Schachter-Shalomi would become leaders of Jewish Renewal, which defines itself as "a worldwide, transdenominational movement" that is "rooted in a Midrashic response to Torah, drawing on ancient wisdom without getting stuck in it." Equally indebted to Kabbalah, neo-Hasidism, ecology, feminism, and the peace movement, Jewish Renewal offers its worshippers a profoundly physical experience, filled with movement and song.

"Under Reb Zalman's influence," writes Rodger Kamenetz in *Stalking Elijah: Adventures with Today's Jewish Mystical Masters,* "Jewish renewal settings became laboratories doing 'R and D work in davennology.'" (*Daven* is the Yiddish word for "pray.")

> Some experiments looked pretty far out: one morning some folks in *tallises* davened knee-deep in the swimming pool for water prayer. . . . But these experiments responded to the diversity of our individual paths. I came to Jewish renewal after contact with Buddhist teachings; my fellow *kallah*-niks [Kamenetz is describing a Jewish Renewal retreat or *kallah* (literally "gathering")] had sojourned in Zen temples, Hindu ashrams, Sufi dancing circles, and Native American sweat lodges or nourished themselves with Jungian psychology, psychosynthesis, Gurdjieff, and New Age philosophers. To the *kallah* came teachers and social workers, doctors and lawyers, professors of humanities and research biologists, and rabbinical students from every denomination. Also people who channeled angels, told fortunes with palm and crystals, who thought they were psychics or healers and maybe

were. Just as sentimentality offers a necessary edge to feeling, belief space includes a wide swath of credulity. We all needed each other.

We have traveled a long way from Herr Professor Scholem's scholarly austerities, but not such a great distance at all from the Besht's disciples turning cartwheels while they prayed or from Rabbi Nachman of Breslov's medical advice ("looking at an *etrog* [a citron fruit] is a cure for eyestrain"; "if one becomes suddenly mute, a kosher slaughterer's knife should be passed over his lips"; "rainwater is a cure for impotence"); or from the traditional belief that Eleazar of Worms traveled instantaneously from Germany to Spain via *kefisat derekh* ("the leaping of the road") to teach Nachmanides the secrets of Kabbalah, or that Shimon bar Yochai and his son lived off a miraculous carob tree in their cave for thirteen years—or the idea that knowing someone's name gives you supernatural power over them. A wide swath of credulity indeed.

As Rabbi Kook wrote in his *Orot ha-Kodesh* (Light of Holiness), "The fierce power of imagination is a gift from God. Joined with the grandeur of the mind, the potency of inference, ethical depth, and the natural sense of the divine, imagination becomes an instrument for the holy spirit."

# 5

## JEWISH MAGIC:
## AMULETS, DEMONS,
## AND THE USE OF NAMES

*Instructions for arousing love, taken from medieval German Jewish spells:*

*[For a man]: "Place a small copper plate upon which a spell has been incised in a new glass goblet filled with your sweat and hide it in a place in which the woman must pass.*

*[For a woman]: "Take a hot bath, cover the entire body with flour, and perspire profusely; wipe the sweat off with a clean white linen cloth, and wring it into a dish; mix in an egg; cut the nails from hands and feet and the hair from the entire body and burn these to a powder; bake them all together and serve."*

Judaism is unambiguously ambiguous on the subject of magic. In some passages, the Bible categorically deplores it, for instance, the following lines from Deuteronomy 18:12–14:

> Let no one be found among you who consigns his son or
> daughter to the fire, or who is an augur, a soothsayer, a di-
> viner, a sorcerer, one who casts spells, or one who consults

ghosts or familiar spirits, or one who inquires of the dead. For anyone who does such things is abhorrent to the Lord, and it is because of these abhorrent things that the Lord your God is dispossessing them before you. You must be wholehearted with the Lord your God. Those nations that you are about to dispossess do indeed resort to soothsayers and augurs, to you, however, the Lord your God has not assigned the like.

But the Bible never denies the efficacy of magic—even if its practitioners derive their powers from sources other than the one true God. One is left with the impression that if the Lord despises these false gods and the pagans who serve them, he still gives them credit where credit is due.

While a modern person might be quick to dismiss magic altogether as mere superstition, the Bible's vehemence on the subject suggests that neither its existence nor its power was ever in question—if they were, they wouldn't have had to be condemned. One is left wondering why an omnipotent God didn't simply render these lesser spirits (and the pagan priests who invoked them) impotent (never mind how He could have tolerated their existence at all)—and how, given these biblical proscriptions, the later kabbalists were able to reconcile their piety with their magical practice.

There are many possible answers. First and foremost, we need to remember that the God of the Bible is different from the God of Maimonides or Martin Buber. The biblical Jews were only just emerging from polytheism; the world they lived in was filled with spirits and demons and even (though it would have been heretical to say so at a later date) subsidiary deities.

*Ein Sof*—the abstract, infinite God without attributes—is a notion that the Jews of Exodus, who witnessed all manner of wonders, whose leader spoke to God face-to-face, and whose hereditary priests conducted sanguinary sacrificial rites, would not have been able to make much sense of.

There are many inconsistencies in the Jewish Bible—that's why the rabbinic tradition came to be. And in fact the Talmud interpreted those biblical ordinances against sorcery rather narrowly, understanding them to refer only to *idolatrous* sorcery. So long as they were used for nonidolatrous purposes, the invocation of angels and demons and "the employment of names" were not forbidden. The rabbis had no choice—magical thinking and magical practice were endemic.

Even so, some kabbalists did reject magic (as we have seen with Abraham Abulafia). It's also important to remember that many of the accounts of wonder-working kabbalists that have come down to us must be taken with a grain of salt. For most of its history, the Kabbalah was esoteric—very few noninitiates knew what those wise men were actually up to when they met secretly and exchanged forbidden manuscripts. Tall tales abounded.

"People of the Book" or not, most Jews held on to their folk superstitions (many of which dated back to polytheistic times), and the Jews of the Diaspora were quick to absorb at least some of the beliefs and superstitions of the people they lived among—whether they were Assyrians and Babylonians, Muslim Sufis, Christian Gnostics, or German Catholic peasants. Thus the demoness Lilith, Adam's estranged first wife, who preys on baby boys before they are circumcised and baby girls in their first twenty days of life, and who seduces men in their sleep, is a Judaized version of the Assyrian wind spirit called a *lilitu*. In primitive times, pagan Teutonic women had made offerings of their hair to a fertility goddess known as *Berchta*. Later, a braided loaf of bread, known as a *Berchisbrod*, was substituted for their actual tresses. Scholars still argue about whether this is the origin of the braided *challah* eaten on the Sabbath, but it isn't a far-fetched suggestion. So too did medieval German Jews come to believe in dragons, vampires, werewolves, and even witches with disheveled hair who flew about at night and turned themselves into cats.

If Jewish people didn't always know what the kabbalists were doing, their frequently hostile, superstitious, and paranoid Christian neighbors knew even less (but assumed the worst). The Christian Cabala and Hermetic Qabala that developed in the late Middle Ages were much more concerned with magic than their Jewish counterparts (much of their magic is specifically Arab rather than Jewish in origin); also, Christians often projected their own forbidden practices onto the hated Jews. That was certainly the case with satanism. Virtually all of the satanic horrors that the Inquisition condemned—the sacrifice of infants, the desecration of Christian iconography (upside-down crosses and the like)—were wrongly imputed to the Jews. This is almost certainly how the blood libels, the manifestly false accusations of Jewish ritual murders that began in medieval times and continued into the twentieth century, began. There is no possible source in Jewish scripture, custom, or belief for the idea of mixing human blood with Passover matzoh—the laws of kashruth reflect an instinctive abhorrence of blood. Most likely the idea originated in the Christian imagination as a desecration of the Eucharist.

Kabbalah emerged in a Europe that was haunted by spirits

and demons. Ghosts roamed the roads at night; demons en-joyed frequent sexual intercourse with sleeping humans in the hope of giving birth to human/spirit hybrids, who held high status in the spirit world. Every living thing (even every blade of grass) had supernatural entities associated with it. Whether you believed in the transmigration of souls or not, cemeteries were known to be crowded with ghosts.

You didn't have to be a kabbalist to know that you were in constant danger of supernatural attack. Prayers and amulets, salt and spices all provided protection; as did the simple expedients of avoiding praise and speaking in circumlocutions (so as not to attract the invidious attentions of demons); the subject of illness was avoided in conversation so as not to prematurely pique the interest of the angel of death. Dream divination goes all the way back to Joseph in the Bible, astrology and palmistry had been practiced since before the destruction of the Temple. Amulets—objects with supernatural powers that were worn on the person or kept nearby—like a fox's tail to sweep away demons, a red coral necklace to ward off the evil eye, or any of a variety of gems (for instance rubies to prevent miscarriage, beryl to aid the digestion)—had been popular since biblical times. Written amulets (sometimes on parchment, sometimes on a piece of jewelry) were highly prized as well. Some of them in-cluded long prayers and invocations and lists of appropriate an-gelic intercessors, others just symbols, like the six-pointed Star of David (see page 106). Phylacteries, or *tefillin* (the cubes strapped to the head and arms during morning prayer), and *mezuzah*s (the boxes containing the text of the prayer called the *Shema* that Jews attach to their doorposts) are both amulets, of course.

There is nothing intrinsically Jewish about sympathetic magic (magic that works by using a surrogate for the person or thing you wish to affect—like sticking pins into a voodoo doll), but neither were Jews immune to its attractions. The following passages are from Moses Gaster's nineteenth-century translation of *The Sword of Moses,* written in Hebrew and Aramaic during the nine hundreds. The numerals in the text refer to the names of angels or God that are listed in an earlier part of the work, along with their appropriate invocations. We will learn more about the use of divine names momentarily:

> If you wish to kill a man, take mud from the two sides of the river and form it into the shape of a figure, and write upon it the name of the person, and take seven branches from seven strong palm-trees and make a bow from reed [*sic*] with the string of horse-sinew, and place the image in a hollow, and stretch the bow and shoot with it. . . . To send plagues, take [parings?] from seven men and put them into a new potsherd, and go out to the cemetery and say there No. 69, and bury it in a place that is not trodden by horses, and afterwards take the dust from this potsherd and blow it into his face or upon the lintel of his house. To send dreams to your neighbors, write No. 70 upon a plate of silver and place it in the [mouth] of a cock and kill it when it has gone down its mouth, and take it out from the mouth and put it between its legs and bury it at the end of a wall, and put thy foot upon that spot and say thus: "In the name of X, a swift messenger is to go and torment NN in his dreams until he will fulfil my wish."

─────── How Come? ───────

*Is the Star of David a Magical Symbol?*

Yes, but it has been a Jewish symbol per se for only a few hundred years. *Mogen David* literally means "Shield of David," but the symbol dates back to the Bronze Age, when it was common throughout Mesopotamia, India, and even Britain. Its oldest known use by a Jew dates back to the sixth century B.C.E., on a seal belonging to Joshua bar Asayahu; it can be found on a frieze on a synagogue in Capernaum dating from the second or third century C.E. (ironically a pentagram and a swastika appear alongside it). It is unknown what significance, beyond the decorative, it might have had.

Starting in the Middle Age it began to appear on notary seals throughout Europe. Arab sources from this era called it "the Seal of Solomon"—this connects it to an early Greek pseudepigraphic work known as the *Testament of Solomon* (in which Solomon engraved the image on his ring to give him power over demons). Sometime in the Middle Ages, the hexagram began to appear as well on depictions of a magical "Shield of David," which supposedly protected him from his enemies. This shield was first described in the Geonic period, but at that time it was emblazoned with the "Name of 72," plus one of Metatron's names. By medieval times the divine name *Shaddai,* written inside the hexagram, had replaced the seventy-two names. The two names—the Seal of Solomon and the Shield of David—were used interchangeably until 1700 as the symbol became more and more common. In 1354, when the Jews of Prague were granted the right to have their own flag, they emblazoned it with the hexagram; it appears as a printer's mark on many books printed in Prague. Because of the messianic associations of King David, the hexagram became especially popular with followers of Shabbetai Zevi.

When newly emanicpated nineteenth-century Jews were casting about for an equivalent symbol to the cross they chose the *Mogen David*. It began to appear on synagogue walls and on ritual objects; the Rothschilds included it in their coat of arms when they were ennobled in the 1820s. Eastern European Jews, who were long familiar with it as a magical or messianic symbol, were quick to accept it. The founder of modern Zionism, Theodor Herzl, chose it to be the symbol of his movement because of its nonreligious character. Franz Rosenzweig's famous book *Star of Redemption* (1921) midrashically interprets the six-pointed star as representing two triads of ideas that constitute Jewish belief: Creation, Revelation, and Redemption; God, Israel, and the World.

---

The notion that knowing someone's name gives you power over them is a basic tenet of magic—but this is precisely where Kabbalah comes into its own. God brought the universe into being by speaking. God's language is Hebrew: the letters of its alphabet are the building blocks of creation; the numbers that they can be transmuted into reveal the even deeper structures of creation. Since the scriptures are a transcription of God's own voice, the revelation they contain is far deeper than just their verbal content. Hebrew letters and numbers, Hebrew words, biblical verses, and names—of angels, demons, spirits, and especially of God Himself—provide the wonder-worker with a vast arsenal of magical tools.

Rabbi Eleazar of Worms describes a charm that's used against a fever demon named Ochnotinos. You chant "Ochnotinos,

chnotinos, notinos, otinos, tinos, inos, nos, os." The demon's powers will diminish as his name does. Since biblical times, Egyptian sorcerers made magical use of the names of foreign deities whether or not they understood or could even properly pronounce the words of the language, probably on the principle that the more gods you could invoke, the more powerful you would be. This practice (Joshua Trachtenberg, in his classic study *Jewish Magic and Superstition*, calls it *barbarica onomata*) was adapted by Jews and carried on into the Middle Ages. "This was the background of thirteenth-century Jewish name-magic," Trachtenberg observes, "which succeeded in introducing into Judaism a host of pagan and Christian deities and terms, often in the most confused and unrecognizable forms." Trachtenberg observes that medieval Christians did the same thing—at least one of them included Buddha in a list of saints!

The most powerful names that the kabbalists had at their disposal were the secret names of God. The tetragrammaton had been considered too powerful to pronounce since biblical times—the high priest in the Temple would only utter "the ineffable name" out loud once a year. Other divine names, such as *Ehyeh*, or "I shall be," carry tremendous power. To those were added 12- and 42-letter names, as well as names of 8, 10, 14, 16, 18, 21, 22, 32, 60, and 72 letters, syllables, or words, which were derived by complicated formulas. (Not all of the algorithms used by kabbalists are *Gematrical*, that is, based on number equivalents. For instance, with *Notarikon* you make acrostics by arranging words that start with the first or last letters of a biblical verse into a new phrase; with *Temurah* you create anagrams out of chosen letters from a phrase—say, the first letter of the first word and the last letter of the last word, the second letter of the second word and the second-to-last letter of the second-to-last word. You can make almost any words or phrases at all by these methods, including apparently meaningless, unpronounceable ones.) The twenty-two-letter name of God is derived from the Priestly Blessing (Numbers 6:22–27). The forty-two-letter name may have been derived from the first forty-two letters in the Bible. The "holy and awesome seventy-two-part name," the most powerful of all secret names of God, was derived from Exodus 14:19–21:

> The angel of God, who had been going ahead of the Israelite army, now moved and followed behind them; and the pillar of cloud shifted from in front of them and took up a place behind them, and it came between the army of the Egyptians and the army of Israel. Thus there was the cloud with the darkness and it cast a spell upon the night, so that the one could not come near the other all through the night. Then Moses held out his arm over the sea and the Lord drove back the sea with a strong east wind all that night, and turned the sea into dry ground.

This name consists of seventy-two three-letter "words." The first letter of verse 19, the last letter of verse 20, and the first letter of 21 form the first triad; the second letter of 19, the second-to-last of 20, and the second of 21 form the second three letters, and so on. Legend has it that Moses was taught this formula at the burning bush and used it to part the Red Sea. According to the *Sefer Raziel,* a medieval Jewish compendium of magic, "Whoever pronounces this name against a demon, it will vanish; at a conflagration, it will be quenched; over an invalid, he will be healed . . . if it is directed against an enemy, he will die. . . . But whoever pronounces this name while he is in a state of uncleanness and impurity will surely be struck dead." Not to be outdone, the Kabbalah Centre, in an advertisement for a book and card deck called *The Seventy-Two Names of God: Technology for the Soul,* describes it as "the ultimate pill for any and every thing that ails you because it strikes at the DNA level of our soul."

Magical thinking remains a stubbornly persistent feature of Jewish life today (ultra-Orthodox kabbalists in Israel cursed Saddam Hussein during the first Gulf War and Yitzhak Rabin after the Oslo Accords by performing a ritual called "the beating by fire"*; the Web site of a kabbalist/therapist describes how she facilitates past-life regressions; the Kabbalah Centre does a booming business in red string bracelets; my mother never gives someone a present before it's really their birthday), but official, mainstream Judaism has long distanced itself from such superstitions.

The historians, philosophers, and rabbis who rediscovered Judaism's great mystical and spiritual traditions in the first half of the twentieth century had secular educations and values; consequently they accorded less importance to the magical side of Kabbalah than it deserved. Martin Buber focused on Hasidic spirituality and ethics; Gershom Scholem's studies laid a

---

*The Jerusalem Post* described the ceremony thusly: twenty-four black candles are placed on a copper tray and carried into a cave near the tomb of the prophet Samuel. After the candles are lit, a *minyan* (the quorum of ten adult Jews required for formal worship) of fasting kabbalists circle the tray, chanting a curse seven times. The candles are pelted with lead balls and pieces of earthenware until they're snuffed; finally, the shofar is sounded. If the curse is successful, its victim will die and his wife will be given to another man.

greater emphasis on the theosophical, theoretical side of Kabbalah than its ecstatic or practical applications. Until recently, the most intensive research on kabbalistic magic was conducted in the context of the Hermetic and Christian counterparts to Kabbalah.

Some of this is starting to change. As Moshe Idel noted in his introduction to the new edition of Trachtenberg's *Jewish Superstition*, the latest generation of historians has begun to turn its attention from the "official religion or culture" of the people they study to the "esotericism, the minority, sectarian, or sometimes even clandestine phenomena" of popular or folk culture. Women, for so long banned from formal participation in Torah and Talmud study and public prayer, kept many of these "folk" traditions alive; feminist historians will undoubtedly pay closer attention to this side of Jewish life in years to come.

# MEDITATIONS AT THE
# HEART OF KABBALAH

*The thought expands and ascends to its origin, so that when it reaches it,
it ends and cannot ascend any further . . . therefore the pious men of old
raised their thought to its origin while pronouncing the precepts and words
of prayer. . . . Their words became blessed, multiplied, full of influx from
the stage called the "nothingness of thought," just as the waters of a pool
flow on every side when a man sets them free.*

—AZRIEL OF GERONA

Meditation *(hitbonenut)* is at the heart of Kabbalah—whether
as *kavvanah* (concentration) or *dvekut* (cleaving) in prayer, or
through the ecstatic, yogic techniques of the *Merkabah* mystics
and Abraham Abulafia. It can also be intellectual (as in the
contemplation of the *Sefirot* or the intensive study of holy
texts). Rabbi Aryeh Kaplan (1934–1983), a trained physicist
and Orthodox rabbi, who wrote or translated more than fifty
scholarly and popular books in his short life, is often credited
with reviving interest in Jewish meditation outside of the Hasidic community with the publication of his seminal *Jewish
Meditation, Meditation and the Bible,* and *Meditation and Kabbalah* in the 1970s. Following are some very basic, kabbalisti-

cally inspired meditations, some dating back to the time of the
*Zohar*, some as contemporary as the Internet.

## IMAGINE YOU ARE LIGHT

AZRIEL OF GERONA (13TH CENTURY)

Whatever one implants firmly in the mind becomes the essential thing. So if you pray and offer a blessing to God, or if you wish your intention to be true, imagine that you are light. All around you—in every corner and on every side—is light. Turn to your right, and you will find shining light; to your left, splendor, a radiant light. Between them, up above, the light of the Presence. Surrounding that, the light of life. Above it all, a crown of light—crowning the aspirations of thought, illumining the paths of imagination, spreading the radiance of vision. This light is unfathomable and endless.

## THE GATES OF HOLINESS

HAYYIM VITAL (16TH CENTURY)

You must be alone, so that your contemplation not be disturbed. In your mind, cultivate aloneness to the utmost. Strip your body from your soul, as if you do not feel that you are clothed in matter at all—you are entirely soul. The more you strip yourself of material being, the more powerful your comprehension. If you sense any sound or movement that breaks your meditation or if any material imagining arises within you, then your soul's contemplation will be severed from the upper worlds. You will attain nothing, since supernal holiness does not abide with anyone attached by even a hair to the material realm. Therefore prophecy or the holy spirit is called deep sleep, dream, or vision. To sum up, even if you are worthy for the holy spirit to rest upon you, if you do not train yourself to completely strip your soul from your body, the spirit will not rest upon you. This is the secret reason that a band of prophets has timbrels, flutes, and other instruments, for through the sweetness of melody, aloneness descends upon them and they strip their souls. Then the musicians stop the melody, and the prophets remain in that supernal state of union and they prophesy.

If you wish to attain aloneness, you must first return to God from having strayed and missed the mark. Be careful not to miss again. Train yourself to eliminate negative habits such as anger, depression, impatience, and chatter.

If you wish to attain aloneness and to receive the holy spirit, regard every insight you gain and every light you perceive as darkness. When you see that you have attained a little, concentrate more deeply in your meditation, until you experience a pure spirit speaking within you words of Torah, wisdom, devotion, purity, and holiness—on its own, without your will. Having attained this, impel yourself to draw forth the holy spirit often, until you weaken and verge on fainting. Then strengthen yourself and pray this prayer with perfect intention:

"Master of all the worlds! To you it is revealed and known that I am not engaged in all of this for my own glory, but rather for the glory of your name, for the glory of the oneness of your being, so that I will know you, how to serve you and bless your name. Enable me to search for you, discover you. Strengthen me, embolden me. Enlighten my eyes lest I sleep the sleep of death. Create a pure heart for me, O God, rejuvenate within me a steadfast spirit."

Draw forth the spirit until you see and know for certain that it is bound to you perpetually, inseparably, engraved within you.

Sanctify your limbs and adorn them with good deeds, making yourself into a throne for the divine presence, your body an ark for the *Shekhinah*. When you do a good deed, you sanctify yourself.

## A MEDITATION ON THE TREE OF LIFE

TAMAR FRANKIEL (CONTEMPORARY)

The Tree of Life has turned out to be central for me. (Here I'm speaking from my experience not on the basis of other authorities.) Here's an example: I visualize the Tree as though imprinted on and located "in" my body. The upper three *Sefirot* are at the head (crown, right and left temples); the next three are at shoulders and heart; the next three at hips and genitals; the tenth at the feet. I visualize these lighting up from top to bottom and right to left: crown, right temple, left temple, right shoulder, etc. The idea is to imagine Divine light pouring through each of these energy centers in your own body; you are the vessel. Sometimes it is helpful first to visualize a cleansing of each of the centers—with gentle waters, or with wind—before imagining them being filled with light.

Another variation is saying the Priestly Blessing, which has three verses, in coordination with a "visualization" of Divine energy filling each of the three triangles (head, upper torso, lower torso), ending with the word "peace" as the energy reaches the feet.

> Yiv'verekhekhah v'yishm 'rekhah
> *The Lord bless you and protect you*
> Ya'er Adonai panav eilekhah v'khumekhah
> *The Lord deal kindly and graciously with you*
>
> Yisah Adonai panav eilekhah va-yasem l'khah shalom
> *The Lord bestow His favor upon you and grant you peace*
>
> NUMBERS 6:24–26

Another variation is to use color with the ten *Sefirot*. There are a number of color systems used by kabbalists; the one I use is a little complicated and uses information from non-Jewish sources as well.

Prayer, by the way, is another story. In the traditional prayer book, which is thoroughly infused with mysticism, one works one's way upward through the Four Worlds. (Prayer is called *Avodah* which is translated "service," "labor," or simply, hard work!)

Meditation for me is a way of becoming receptive and allowing myself to experience Divine loving kindness, which is everpresent. Some people tell me they contemplate different areas of the Tree of Life depending on what's going on with them (e.g., emotional or physical problems). I find that puts too much of personal will into the meditation, and I have plenty of that in the rest of my life already!

—POSTED ON BELIEFNET

## A *SHEMA* MEDITATION

A good meditation to start out with is the *Shema* meditation described in Aryeh Kaplan's classic 1985 text *Jewish Meditation*. *Shema*, which is Hebrew for "hear," is the word that begins Judaism's holiest prayer, the fundamental affirmation of Jewish faith in one God—*shema yisrael adonai eloheinu adonai ehod*, "Hear oh Israel, the Lord Our God, the Lord is One."

Inhale silently, and exhale "shh." Then inhale again silently, and exhale "mmm." Repeat this process, allowing it to draw you deeper and deeper into the "mmm" sound. This practice helps the meditator achieve a meditative state. Another meditation to experiment with involves focusing upon a *Shiviti*, a line from Psalm 16 inscribed on a plaque that Jews traditionally focused on before meditation, to help them reach another state of consciousness. The Hebrew verb *shiviti* ("I place") comes from verse 8 of the psalm: *"Shiviti Adonai l'negdi tamid/*I am ever mindful of the Lord's presence."

—POSTED ON BELIEFNET

## A MEDITATION ON GOD'S NAME
ARTHUR GREEN (CONTEMPORARY)

Prepare yourself for meditation. Sit with eyes closed, breathing quietly. When you are ready, begin to breathe through your open mouth. Without sound, shape your lips just slightly to form a "y"-like breath on the intake. As you breathe out, the voiceless "H"-sound will be quite natural. On the next breath, form your lips in just a slightly different way to breathe in a "w."

Then breathe out again, "h." Do not recite the names of the letters *("yod, he"),* but just silently breathe in and out the sound of each letter. Thus you are breathing the name of God.

Nothing could be simpler. God is as natural as the breath of life. You are breathing the name of God. Continue, breathing in and out through the mouth, gently forming the "y" and "w" on the intake breaths. As you enter into the process, you may carry the images of the *Sefirot* with you in your breathing. On "y," reach inward toward *hokhmah,* source of all, transcendent mystery. On "h," *hokhmah* breathes out to *binah,* birthing all the energies. Your "w" reconcentrates these as the six directions, or "days," of activity all come together as the "male" principle, entering again into "h" as *Shekhinah,* God throughout the world and within your soul.

Breathe in, breathe out. Y-H-W-H. When you are ready, let go of the concentrated oral breaths. Breathe naturally, but continue to be aware. This is the moment to acknowledge that all breath is the breathing in and out of God's name, that to live, by the simple fact of breathing, is to recite the name of God. This is the conclusion of the psalmist: "Every breath praises God. Halleluyah!"

### A MEDITATION ON RAISING HOLY SPARKS

DAVID COOPER (CONTEMPORARY)

The infinite primordial light spread radiance on everything and as it spread to all sides, the light shot out sparks. God stored these away for the righteous. Why?

So that the righteous could bring forth fruit from these sparks. Thus it indeed happened that they brought forth fruit in the world. For Abraham and Sarah "made souls" (Genesis 12:5). Just as they made souls from the Holy Side [the "good" side of creation], so too did they make souls from the Other Side [the "evil" side of creation]. For if this influence of the Other Side were not in this world, there would be nothing to overcome [and therefore no real free choice to do good].—*Zohar Shemot* 147b

The Baal Shem Tov teaches that all things have within them holy sparks. We have to learn to see through the hard shells of creation to discover holy sparks hidden inside so that we can raise them up to their origin and ultimately attain messianic consciousness. The following is a guided meditation to give us ideas for identifying these sparks and what we have to do to raise them up.

1. Sit quietly with your eyes closed, attending the breath, noticing the body. Do this for five minutes.
2. Allow yourself to think of someone that you know quite well, and to think about no more than three of his or her personality traits that you really like—the three most likeable, positive things that you know about this person.
3. Now allow yourself to think of one or more attributes that you really find unpleasant about this person, something that makes you uncomfortable that you wish could be changed. If there are more than one, pick the one that you dislike the most and focus on it. On the other hand,

if you are unable to identify anything unpleasant, choose a different person for this exercise, and then repeat steps 2 and 3.

4. Look deep within yourself to see if you can determine what it is about the unpleasant trait or characteristic that really bothers you. What do you identify with it? What kind of fear does it raise in you? It might help to imagine what it would be like if you, yourself, had this trait. How would you relate to it and how would others relate to you? Use your imagination. Imagine yourself with this trait and see how it feels.

5. Imagine yourself with this trait that is unlikeable and see if you can discover within it something useful, something nourishing, something that it accomplishes. Imagine that it is a gift, this trait, a gift from the Divine. When you are able to open the gift and see deep within, you will discover a profound truth. So what is the truth hidden deep within this characteristic that you find so uncomfortable?

6. Now that you have discovered that this attribute contains something of truth from the Divine, once again allow yourself to reflect upon the person who has this trait. Let yourself now experience this person with this characteristic or attribute, noticing how you feel about him or her.

7. You will probably notice that your feelings have changed somewhat. If so, this is called "raising the sparks." Stay with these feelings for a little while and notice how those inner edges of criticism and judgment soften when your

understanding deepens about the sparks hidden within everything.

Do this exercise again for others with different personality traits. Notice that there is always some kind of redeeming spark to be found in almost everything. After completing these meditations, reflect on them as often as you remember to do so. Especially think about this when you encounter people in daily life who have unpleasant characteristics and see if you can modify your reactions on the spot. This is what it takes to identify holy sparks and raise them up. Do this meditation exercise whenever you feel yourself becoming alienated and critical. It is another technique for softening the heart.

# A MINI-ANTHOLOGY OF KABBALAH

### FROM *THE WORK OF THE CHARIOT*
(3RD CENTURY C.E.)

Rabbi Ishmael said: When my rabbi, Rabbi Nehunia ben ha-Kanah, heard that I have stood facing heaven and identified every single angel who is in every single palace, He said to me: Why did you identify the angels who are positioned in the gates of each palace? I told him: I did not do it in order to praise myself, but in order to praise the king of the universe. Rabbi Ishmael said: My rabbi, Rabbi Nehunia ben ha-Kanah told me: The true torah which Aharon the priest acquired is what was your support, and [because of it] you did not suffer as a result [of disclosing] this secret. But if you wish to make use of this secret you should fortify yourself with eight prayers which I shall recite. At that time he arranged before me the prayers, each one including twelve letters from the name of the living, eternally existing God, the revered God who is sanctified and who is inhabiting all the vistas of the celestial realms. Rabbi Ishmael said: Since Rabbi Nehunia ben ha-Kanah arranged before me these prayers, I have been praying every day by the names in each of them, when ascending and when descending, and all the limbs of my body were comforted.

## FROM THE *ZOHAR*

(12TH CENTURY)

### The Process of Emanation

*In the beginning* (Gen. 1:1)—At the very beginning the king made engravings in the supernal purity. A spark of blackness emerged in the sealed within the sealed, from the mystery of *Ein-Sof*, a mist within matter, implanted in a ring, no white, no black, no red, no yellow, no color at all. When he measured with the standard of measure, he made colors to provide light. Within the spark, in the innermost part, emerged a source, from which the colors are painted below, and it is sealed among the sealed things of the mystery of *Ein-Sof*. It penetrated, but did not penetrate, its air; it was not known at all, until from the pressure of its penetration—a single point shone, sealed, supernal. Beyond this point nothing is known, and so it is called *reshit* (beginning, genesis): the first word of all.

*And they that are wise shall shine as the brightness (zohar) of the firmament, and they that turn the many to righteousness as the stars forever and ever* (Dan. 12:3). Zohar, sealed among the sealed things, made contact with its air, which touched, but did not touch, the point. Then the "beginning" (*reshit*) extended itself and made a palace for itself, for glory and praise. There it sowed the holy seed (*zera*) in order to beget offspring for the benefit of the world.

### Of All the Trees in the Garden Thou Shall Surely Eat

We have learnt that at that moment Samael came down from heaven riding on this serpent, and all creatures saw his form and fled before him. They then entered into conversation with the woman, and the two brought death into the world. Of a surety Samael brought curses on the world through Wisdom and destroyed the first tree that God had created in the world. This responsibility rested on Samael until another holy tree came, namely Jacob, who wrested the blessings from him, in order that Samael might not be blessed above and Esau below. For Jacob was the reproduction of Adam, and he had the same beauty as Adam. Therefore as Samael withheld blessings from the first tree, so Jacob, who was such another tree as Adam, withheld blessings, both upper and lower, from Samael; and in doing so Jacob but took back his own.

This serpent is the evil tempter and the angel of death. It is because the serpent is the angel of death that it brought death to the world.

"With this tree God created the world; eat therefore of it, and ye shall be like God, knowing good and evil, for through this knowledge he is called God." What he said was that God ate of the tree and so built the world. "Therefore," he went on, "eat you of it and you shall create worlds."

With reference to the dictum quoted above, that God prohibited to Adam idolatry, injustice, murder, incest, and so forth, why should all this have been necessary, seeing that Adam was still alone in the world? The answer is that all these prohibitions had reference to the tree alone, and were applicable to it. For whoever takes of it causes separation and associates himself with the lower hordes which are attached to it. He renders himself guilty of idolatry, murder, and adultery. Of idolatry, because he acknowledges the superior chieftains; of bloodshed, because that is inspired by this tree, which is of the side of *Gevurah* (Force), under the charge of Samael; and of adultery, because the tree is of the female principle and is called "woman," and it is forbidden to make an appointment with a woman without her husband, for fear of suspicion of adultery.

Now God formed [Adam] with both good and evil inclination—with the good inclination for himself, and the evil inclination to turn towards the female. Esoterically speaking, we learn from here that the North is always attracted to the female and attaches itself to her, and therefore she is called *isha* (i.e., *esh* he, fire of he). Observe this. The good inclination and the evil inclination are in harmony only because they share the female, who is attached to both, in this way: first the evil inclination sues for her and they unite with one another, and when they are united the good inclination, which is joy, rouses itself and draws her to itself, and so she is shared by both and reconciles them. Hence it is written, "and the Lord God formed man," the double name being made responsible both for the good and the evil inclination. As we have explained, male and female, together and not separated, so as to turn face-to-face.

The use of the word "[dust of the] ground" (*adamah*) here must be explained. When the wife is joined with the husband she is called by the name of the husband; thus the correlatives *ish* (man) and *ishah*, *tzaddik* (righteous one), and *zedek*, *'ofer* (buck) and *'efar*, *zebi* (hart), and *Tibia*. So, too, with the words *asher* (which) and *asherah*. It says, "Thou shalt not plant thee an *Asherah* (grove) of any kind of tree beside the altar of the Lord thy God which (*asher*) thou shalt make thee." Are we to suppose that anywhere else it is permitted? The truth is that the *Hi* is called *Asherah,* after the name of its spouse, *Asher,* and the meaning of the verse is therefore: "thou shalt not plant another *asherah* by the side of the altar which is established upon this."

Observe that throughout the Scriptures the worshippers of the sun are called servants of *Baal* and the worshippers of the moon servants of *Asherah;* hence the combination "to *Baal* and *Asherah."* If this is so (that *Asherah* is the name of the *Hi*), why is it not used as a sacred name? The reason is that this name brings to mind the words of Leah, "happy am I, for the daughters will call me happy (*ishruni*)," but this one is not "called happy" by other nations, and another is set up in its place; nay more, it is written, "all that honored her despise her" (Lam. i, 8).

It is incumbent on a man to be ever "male and female," in order that his faith may be firm, and that the *Shekhinah* may never depart from him. What, then, you will say, of a man who goes on a journey and, being absent from his wife, is no longer "male and female"? His remedy is to pray to God before he starts his journey, while he is still "male and female" in order to draw to himself the presence of his Master. When he has offered his prayer and thanksgiving and the *Shekhinah* rests on him, then he can depart, for through his union with the *Shekhinah* he has become "male and female" in the country as he was "male and female" in the town, as it is written: "Righteousness (*zedek,* the female of *tzaddik*) shall go before him and shall place his footsteps on the way". . . . Observe this. All the time that a man is on his travels he should be very careful of his actions, in order that the celestial partner may not desert him and leave him defective, through lacking the union with the female. If this was necessary when his wife was with him, how much more so is it necessary when a heavenly partner is attached to him? All the more so since this heavenly partner guards him on the way all the time until he returns home. When he does reach home again, it is his duty to give his wife some pleasure, because it is she who procured for him this heavenly partner. It is his duty to do this for two reasons. One is that this pleasure is a religious pleasure, and one which gives joy to the *Shekhinah* also, and what is more, by its means he spreads peace in the world, as it is written, "thou shalt know that thy tent is in peace, and thou shalt visit thy fold and not sin" (Job v, 24). (Is it a sin, it may be asked, if he does not visit his wife? The answer is that it is so because he thereby derogates from the honor of the celestial partner who was joined with him on account of his wife.) The other is that, if his wife becomes pregnant, the celestial partner imparts to the child a holy soul, for this covenant is called the covenant of the Holy One, blessed be He. Therefore he should be as diligent to procure this gladness as to procure the gladness of the Sabbath, which is the partner of the Sages. Hence "thou shalt know that thy tent is in peace," since the *Shekhinah* comes with thee and abides in thy house, and therefore "thou shalt visit thy house and not sin," by performing with gladness the religious duty of conjugal intercourse in the presence of the *Shekhinah*.

In this way the students of the Torah who separate from their wives during the six days of the week in order to devote themselves to study are accompanied by a heavenly partner in order that they may continue to be "male and female." When

Sabbath comes, it is incumbent on them to gladden their wives for the sake of the honor of the heavenly partner, and to seek to perform the will of their Master, as has been said.

Similarly again, if a man's wife is observing the days of her separation, during all those days that he waits for her the heavenly partner is associated with him, so that he is still "male and female." When his wife is purified, it is his duty to gladden her through the glad performance of a religious precept. All the reasons we have mentioned above apply to this case also. The esoteric doctrine is that men of true faith should concentrate their whole thought and purpose on this one (the *Shekhinah*).

You may object that, according to what has been said, a man enjoys greater dignity when he is on a journey than when he is at home, on account of the heavenly partner who is then associated with him. This is not so. For when a man is at home, the foundation of his house is the wife, for it is on account of her that the *Shekhinah* departs not from the house. So our teachers have understood the verse, "and he brought her to the tent of his mother Sarah" (Gen. xxiv, 67), to indicate that with Rebecca the *Shekhinah* came to Isaac's house. Esoterically speaking, the supernal Mother is found in company with the male only when the house is prepared, and the male and female are joined.

### FROM JOSEPH GIKATILLA'S *SHA'AREI ORAH* (THE GATES OF LIGHT)

(13TH CENTURY)

## The Power of the Righteous

The Righteous One stands gazing out at humanity. When he sees human beings engaged in Torah and *mitzvot,* seeking to refine themselves, to conduct themselves in purity, then the Righteous One expands, filling himself with all kinds of flowing emanation from above, to pour into *Shekhinah,* the divine presence, in order to reward those purifying themselves, those cleaving to Torah and *mitzvot.* Thus, the entire world is blessed by those righteous humans, and *Shekhinah* is likewise blessed through them.

But if humans defile themselves by distancing themselves from Torah and *mitzvot,* by perpetrating evil, injustice, and violence, then the Righteous One stands to gaze at what they have done. When he sees, he gathers and contracts himself, ascending higher and higher. Then the flow of all the channels ceases, and *Shekhinah* is left dry and empty, lacking all good.

One who understands this secret understands the immense power a human has to build and to destroy. Now, come and see the power of the righteous: they can unite all the *Sefirot,* harmonizing the upper and the lower worlds.

## FROM MOSES CORDOVERO'S *OR NE'ERAV*
## (THE PLEASANT LIGHT)

(16TH CENTURY)

### Ein Sof *and the* Sefirot

First, you should know that the Creator, *Ein Sof,* is the cause of causes, one without a second, one that cannot be counted. Change and mutability, form and multiplicity, do not apply to it. The word "one" is used metaphorically, since the number one stands on its own and is the beginning of all numbers. Every number is contained with it potentially, while it inheres in every number in actuality.

The Creator is called one from this aspect: *Ein Sof* is present in all things in actuality, while all things are present in it potentially. It is the beginning and cause of everything. In this way oneness has been ascribed to the Creator; nothing can be added to this oneness or subtracted from it. *Ein Sof* is necessary being, just as the number one is necessary for all numbers, since without it no number can exist. If the number one were nullified, all numbers would be nullified, whereas if the numbers were nullified, the number one would not. Such is the power of one.

So it is with the Creator of all, the one who acts and sustains existence. If an action were nullified, the actor would not be nullified, since *Ein Sof* does not need anything. If existence were nullified, *Ein Sof* would not be nullified, since it does not need space and exists on its own.

Furthermore, you should know that *Ein Sof* emanated its *Sefirot,* through which its actions are performed. They serve as vessels for the actions deriving from *Ein Sof* in the world of separation and below. In fact, its existence and essence spread through them.

These qualities possess unerasable names. *Keter* (Crown) is named Ehyeh; *Hokhmah* (Wisdom) is named Yah; *Binah* (Understanding) is named YHVH with the vowels of Elohim; *Hesed* (Love) is named El; *Gevurah* (Power) is named Elohim; *Tif'eret* (Beauty) is named YHVH; *Netzah* (Eternity) is named *Tseva'ot*; *Yesod* (Foundation) is named *Shaddai* or *El Hai*; *Malkhut* (Kingdom) is named *Adonai*.

These names are the *Sefirot*. It is not that the names are merely ascribed to the *Sefirot*; rather, the names *are* the *Sefirot*. These *Sefirotic* names are names of *Ein Sof*, according to its actions.

*Ein Sof* is not identical with *Keter*, as many have thought. Rather, *Ein Sof* is the cause of *Keter; Keter* is caused by *Ein Sof*, cause of causes. *Ein Sof* is the primal cause of all that exists; there is no cause higher than it. *Keter* is the first to derive from it. From *Keter* the rest of emanation is drawn forth. This does not contradict the fact that *Keter* is counted as one of the *Sefirot*. It is reckoned as one of the ten, considered similar to the emanated ones. On account of its loftiness, however, *Keter* does not reveal itself in the emanated totality of ten. The decade is kept complete by including *Da'at* (Knowledge) in place of *Keter*.

It is inappropriate to say of *Ein Sof* "blessed be he," "glorified be he," "praised be he," or similar expressions since it cannot be blessed, praised, or glorified by another. Rather it is the one who blesses, praises, glorifies, and animates from the first point of its emanation to the farthest. Before the formation of the universe, it had no need of emanation. It was concealed in its holy, pure simplicity. No letter, vowel, or image can be applied to it, for even *Keter*, the beginning of emanation, is devoid of name and image in letter or vowel. How much more so with *Ein Sof*, whom we cannot depict, of whom we cannot speak, of whom we cannot posit either judgment or compassion, excitement or anger, change or limit, sleep or motion, or any quality whatsoever, either prior to the emanation or now.

At the very beginning, *Ein Sof* emanated the subtle emanation, namely, ten *Sefirot*, noetic forms—from its essence, uniting with it. It and they together constitute a complete union. These *Sefirot* are souls, which clothe themselves in the ten *Sefirot* called by name, which serve as vessels for the ten essences. Within these ten named *Sefirot* are found judgment and compassion and the aforementioned actions, which we would not ascribe to *Ein Sof*.

Before these qualities emanated, they were utterly concealed within *Ein Sof*, utterly united with it. No image can be applied to them—not even a point; rather, they were united with it. Afterward, *Ein Sof* emanated one point from itself, one emanation. This is *Keter*, called *Ayin*, Nothingness, on account of its extreme subtlety, its cleaving to its source, such that being cannot be posited of it. From *Keter* a second point emanated in a second revelation. This is *Hokhmah* (Wisdom), called *Yesh*, Being, for it is the beginning of revelation and existence. It is called *yesh me-ayin*, "being from nothingness." Because it is the beginning of being and not being itself, it required a third point to reveal what exists. This is *Binah* (Understanding).

From these three *Sefirot* emerged the six dimensions of providence, the *Sefirot* from *Hesed* (Love) and below. First, *Hesed* from *Hokhmah*; then *Gevurah* (Power) emanated from *Binah*; then *Tif'eret* (Beauty) emanated from *Keter*. The revelation of all three of these came about through *Binah*, but the essential roots of *Hesed* and *Tif'eret* derived from *Hokhmah* and *Keter* respectively. Hidden within these three were *Netzah* (Eternity), *Hod* (Splendor), and *Yesod* (Foundation). *Netzah* was revealed from *Hesed*, *Hod* from *Gevurah*, and *Yesod* from *Tif'eret*. *Malkhut* (Kingdom) emanated along with the six dimensions.

The process of emanation can be pictured in three different ways, each of which is true. Either one after the other: *Keter, Hokhmah, Binah, Hesed* . . . to *Malkhut*. Or else *Keter, Tif'eret, Yesod,* and *Malkhut* constitute one point, emanating to the end of *Malkhut*, while *Hokhmah, Hesed,* and *Netzah* constitute a second point, emanating until *Netzah;* and *Binah, Gevurah,* and *Hod* constitute a third point, emanating until *Hod*. Alternatively, *Keter, Hokhmah,* and *Binah*, followed by *Hesed, Gevurah,* and *Tif'eret,* followed by *Netzah, Hod,* and *Yesod*. *Malkhut* is the entirety.

Among the kabbalists, the most widely accepted depiction of the *Sefirot* is as follows: *Keter, Hokhmah,* and *Binah* in the form of a triangle. Beneath them, also in the form of a triangle, *Hesed, Gevurah,* and *Tif'eret,* followed by another triangle of *Netzah, Hod,* and *Yesod*. Centered beneath them is *Malkhut*. The upper *Sefirot* need the lower ones, and the lower *Sefirot* need the upper ones. So the power of the lower *Sefirot* is in the upper ones, and the power of the upper *Sefirot* is in the lower ones. All of them need *Ein Sof*, while it needs none of them.

These *Sefirot* have no specific location, though we depict them in such a way as to make them fathomable. In truth, though, *Ein Sof* is the location of its *Sefirot*, and *Keter* is the location of nine *Sefirot*, and *Hokhmah* is the location of eight, and *Binah* is the location of seven, and so on. *Malkhut* is the location of the world of creation, which is the location of the world of formation, which is the location of the world of actualization, until the emanation reaches the earth.

Various channels have been ascribed to these *Sefirot*, signifying the path of the ray of illumination from the first *sefirah* to its recipient, and the pathway from the recipient back to the emanating *sefirah*, so that it can receive. The joining of these two aspects of light constitutes a channel. The various types of channels are actually innumerable. Among them are the following:

One from *Keter* to *Hokhmah*, one from *Keter* to *Binah*, and one from *Keter* to *Tif'eret*, totaling three.

One from *Hokhmah* to *Binah*, one from *Hokhmah* to *Hesed*, one from *Hokhmah* to *Gevurah*, and one from *Hokhmah* to *Tif'eret*, totaling four.

One from *Binah* to *Hesed*, one from *Binah* to *Gevurah*, and one from *Binah* to *Tif'eret*, totaling three.

One from *Hesed* to *Netzah*, one from *Hesed* to *Gevurah*, and one from *Hesed* to *Tif'eret*, totaling three.

One from *Gevurah* to *Hod*, and one from *Gevurah* to *Tif'eret*, totaling two.

One from *Tif'eret* to *Netzah*, one from *Tif'eret* to *Hod*, and one from *Tif'eret* to *Yesod*, totaling three.

One from *Netzah* to *Hod*, and one from *Netzah* to *Yesod*, totaling two.

One from *Hod* to *Yesod*, and one from *Yesod* to *Malkhut*.

*Malkhut* receives solely from *Yesod*, through whom she receives from them all. Without him, she cannot receive from any of them; without her, none of the *Sefirot* can emanate to the lower worlds, for she is the essence of those worlds, conducting them. These are the major channels; their facets are infinite.

The *Sefirot* have the power to perform opposite actions, at times manifesting judgment, at times compassion. They always agree on each action, for each *sefirah* acts only along with all the others, with their consent, through *Malkhut*.

Each *sefirah* is composed of all ten, yet they manifest particular combinations:

Sometimes a combination of three: *Hesed, Din,* and *Rahamim* (Love, Judgment, and Compassion).

Sometimes a combination of four: the three already mentioned and one composed of them all.

Sometimes five: *Hesed, Gevurah, Tif'eret, Netzah,* and *Hod.*

Sometimes six: the six dimensions.

Sometimes seven, the *Sefirot* from *Hesed* to *Malkhut.*

Sometimes eight, including *Binah.*

Sometimes ten, from *Keter* on down, or from *Hokhmah* on down, with *Da'at* (Knowledge) completing the decade.

These various combinations are not what they seem to be, for the *Sefirot* are never less than ten. Rather, all ten combine in these various modes, revealing themselves in illumination.

The origin of Judgment is on high, in the will of the emanator. However, it is concealed, as all of the qualities are concealed and unified within *Keter* and *Ein Sof,* to such an extent that they cannot be considered individual qualities. Similarly, the activity of Judgment is concealed in the first three *Sefirot,* and it is not considered Judgment until its manifestation in *Gevurah.*

It is improper for the seeker to probe the essence of the first three *Sefirot,* since they constitute the Divine Mind, Wisdom, and Understanding. It is also improper to probe the essence of the hidden substance that creates all that exists. Since it is one with its Will, Wisdom, and Understanding—its essential qualities—it is not proper to probe. However, it is not wrong for us to explore from *Hesed* and *Gevurah* on down, for these qualities have been emanated to conduct the beings below. Whoever explores them thoroughly is rewarded for his zeal. Concerning this it is written: "Let the mother go," referring to *Binah* (Understanding); "the children you may take," to search and explore.

The activities of *Hesed* abound; we will mention here what is apt for the seeker. First, grace—as indicated by its name—benefiting us, being good to us. Also, nullifying the power of the aliens, who accuse and vex us. The effects of this quality are found in all things that partake of whiteness, such as gems whose color is white, whose virtue derives from *Hesed*. Among its actions is love. Although love is aroused by the left, its essential purpose is on the right. Another of its actions is drawing a person toward wisdom through the power of *Hokhmah*, above on the right. Another is including *Gevurah* within itself in order to execute judgment tinged with love.

Among the actions of *Gevurah* are harsh judgment, as indicated by its name. It is a lash to discipline humanity. From here stem all the aliens that seduce and denounce. Its effects are found in all things that partake of the mystery of redness and heat, such as fire and the power of gems whose color is red, whose virtue is striking terror. Yet, as we have noted, love is also aroused by this quality. Wealth and sustenance, too, emanate from here, with the help of *Binah*, above. Every time that God listens to a prayer or a cry of distress, it is through this quality, with the help of *Binah*.

Among the actions of *Tif'eret* are beauty and splendor, as attested by its name. The reason is that splendor and beauty are composed of white and red, as it is written, "My beloved is white and ruddy." Within the mystery of this quality are all things compounded of red and white, fire and water, warmth and wetness, judgment and grace. Also derived from here is the color yellow in gems—like the yellow of the yolk of an egg. All of these emanate from this quality, and their virtues derive from its power. The Torah and the study of Torah both depend on *Tif'eret*. The birth of children depends on the upper *Sefirot*, while its locus is here. The manna descended to Israel from this quality. Souls emanate from here as well, through the mysterious union of this quality with *Malkhut*. Such union takes place between these two *Sefirot*, as well as between *Hokhmah* and *Binah*, but between none of the others.

*Hokhmah* and *Binah* are called man and woman, father and mother. Just as human sexual union requires the medium of genitalia so above, these two qualities unite by means of the mystery of primordial *Da'at*, which mediates between father and mother. This union maintains and renews the *Sefirot*, which are continually revitalized through their root, sunk deep within *Binah* and *Hokhmah*. The soul, which derives from *Binah*, shares in this renewal. However, every union requires an arousal below, and the arousal of *Binah* stems from *Malkhut*.

This manner of union may be found in *Tif'eret* and *Malkhut*, who are male and female, groom and bride, lower father and mother, son and daughter of the upper couple, king and queen, the Holy One, blessed be he, and *Shekhinah*. All these are metaphors. Their union, however, requires an arousal from the lower world, from the souls of the righteous.

Foreplay ushers in the union. There is embrace at the hands of *Hesed* and *Gevurah*, as intimated in the Song of Songs: "His left hand beneath my head, his right arm embracing me." This implies that the emanation of *Hesed* flows into *Tif'eret*, uniting with it. Then *Tif'eret* flows into *Gevurah*, uniting with it. Now the groom is joined with both his arms. Then he receives the bride with his left arm, and *Gevurah* extends to *Malkhut*, emanating to her. Then the abundance of *Hesed*, the right arm, flows to her. Thus the left is below, and the right embraces above.

Accompanying the union is the aspect of the kiss. Undoubtedly, this kiss is the cleaving of spirit to spirit, the mystery of the union of the inner essence of the *Sefirot*, illuminating one another through the mystery of the mouth, *Malkhut* being in *Tif'eret*, *Tif'eret* in *Malkhut*.

The benefits of this union are immense. From it derive male souls from the male side and female souls from the female side. Accompanying this union are *Netzah* and *Hod*, the two testicles of the male, along with *Yesod*, the mystery of the covenant. Thus the union is enacted.


### THE BAAL SHEM TOV OPENS THE GATE
(18TH CENTURY)

Once, on the eve of Yom Kippur, the Besht envisioned a great threat in heaven directed against the people of Israel, that the Oral Torah [The Talmud] will be removed from them. The Besht grieved very much all that day, the eve of Yom Kippur. In the evening, when the whole town came to him to receive a blessing, he gave it to one person or two, and then said that he could not continue to bless them because of his deep sorrow. He then went to the synagogue, and admonished the people, and then he fell down in front of the holy ark, cried and said: *Vay*, for they want to take the Torah away from us, how can we survive among the nations even half a day. And his anger was directed against the Rabbis, for, he said, it was their fault, for they invent lies and false positions. And he said that all the sages of the Talmud will be brought to trial. Then he went to the *bet midrash*, and said more admonishing words, and they prayed the *kol nidrey*, and after *kol nidrey* he said that the threat is growing stronger. He told all the leaders of the prayers to make haste, because it was the custom that he himself would lead the concluding prayer of the day, the *ne'ilah*, and he wanted to do it long before sunset. Before the *ne'ilah* he started to say words of admonishment and cried, and he put his head way back on the praying-table and moaned and shouted. Then he began to pray the silent eighteen benedictions, and then started the loud repetition of the prayer.

It was his custom always on the High Holidays not to look at the prayer-book, but the Rabbi, Rav Yekil of Mezhibuzh, would read from the prayer-book the hymn, standing before him, and the Besht used to repeat the words after him. When he reached the words: "Open a gate for us," or the words "open the gates of heaven," when Rav Yekil said it and repeated it, he heard that the Besht was not repeating after him, so he stopped and remained silent. The Besht then began to move in a terrifying way, he bent himself backwards until his head was close to his knees. The people in the synagogue were afraid that he might fall down. They wanted to help him and hold him up, but they were afraid. They notified Rabbi Ze'ev Kutzes, of blessed memory, and he came and looked at his face and motioned to them not to touch him. His eyes were protruding, and his voice sounded like that of an ox being slaughtered. He remained in this state for about two hours. Suddenly he woke up, straightened himself at his stand and prayed very quickly and finished the prayer.

Later that evening, after the holiday of Yom Kippur was concluded, everybody came to see him, for that was the custom always. They asked him what happened to that threat, and he told them:

When I was standing for the *ne'ilah* prayer, I could pray [without difficulty], and I ascended from one world to the other without meeting any obstacles, during all the silent eighteen benedictions. But when the loud repetition started, I still went on, and I reached one palace, and I had to enter only one final gate before I would stand before the Holy Name Blessed be He. In that palace I found prayers of fifty years which could not ascend. Now, because on this Yom Kippur the prayers were said with great intention, all the prayers ascended, and each prayer was sparkling like the brilliant dawn. I asked those prayers: Why did you not ascend before? They said that they were ordered to wait for Your Highness to lead us. I told them: Come with me. The gate was open. And he told the people of his town that the gate was as large as the whole hall. When we started to walk with all the prayers an angel came and closed the door and put a lock on the gate, and he told them that the lock was as large as all of the town of Mezhibuzh. I started to move the lock around, trying to open it, and could not. So I ran to my teacher and beseeched him and said: The people of Israel are in such great trouble, and now they do not let me enter, for at another time I would not try to force myself to get in. My Rabbi then said: I shall go with you, and if it will be possible to open it, I shall do it. He came and turned the lock and he also could not open it. Then he told me: What can I do for you? I began to complain to my Rabbi: How can you leave me in such a time of trouble? He answered: I do not know what I can do to help you. But you and I can go to the Palace of the Messiah, maybe salvation will come from there. I went, with great tumult, to the Palace of the Messiah. When our righteous Messiah saw me from afar, he told me: Do not shout, and he gave me two letters, and I came to the gate, and thank God I succeeded to open the lock and opened the gate, and I led all the prayers. Because of the great happiness that the elevation of the prayers caused the mouth of the accuser was closed and I even did not have to argue against him. The threat was then cancelled, and all that remained was the impression of that threat.

MARTIN BUBER, FROM *TALES OF THE HASIDIM* (20TH CENTURY)

*Miracles*

The rabbi of Kotzk was told of a wonder-worker who was versed in the secret art of making a robot. "That is unimportant," he said. "But does he know the secret art of making a *hasid*?"

*After Thirty Years*

A certain man had lived in seclusion for thirty years and devoted himself to the Torah. When he returned to the company of men, he heard about Rabbi Yitzhak of Vorki and decided to go to him. On the way there he pictured to himself the joy and honor with which the *tzaddik* would receive so learned a man who had devoted all his efforts to the Torah for so long a time. When he stood in Rabbi Yitzhak's presence, the rabbi said to him: "You're so learned a man and have devoted all your efforts to the Torah for so long a time—surely you know what God says?" The man grew embarrassed and uncertain. Finally he said hesitantly: "God says we should pray and study." The *tzaddik* laughed. "You do not understand my question," he said. The man left in an unhappy frame of mind.

But he went to the *tzaddik* again and again, and each time Rabbi Yitzhak received him with the same words. Then came the day when he made his farewell.

"What are you taking home with you," asked the *tzaddik,* "since you don't know what God says!" Tears rose in the man's eyes as he said: "Rabbi, that is just why I came to you—to learn something!"

"It is written in Jeremiah," said the *tzaddik,* "since you don't know what God says!" Tears rose in the man's eyes as he said: "Rabbi, that is just why I came to you—to learn something!"

"It is written in Jeremiah," said the *tzaddik,* " 'Can any hide himself in secret places'—that means, anyone who locks himself into his room for thirty years and studies the Torah; 'that I shall not see him?'—that means, I may not want to see such a man; 'saith the Lord'—that is what God says."

Moved to the depths of his being, the man stood there, and for a time he could not speak, he could not even think. Then the spirit moved him. "Rabbi," he sighed, "I should like to ask you a question."

"Speak," said the *tzaddik.* "What is the prescribed thing to do," asked the man, "when scraps of a holy book which has been torn fall to the ground?"

"They should be picked up," said the *tzaddik,* "lest they be destroyed."

The man threw himself on the floor. "Rabbi, Rabbi," he cried. "A vessel filled with scraps of the Holy Scriptures lies before you. Do not let them be destroyed!" With both hands the *tzaddik* raised him and seated him at his side. Then he talked to him and helped him with his words.

## The Original Meaning

This is what Rabbi Moshe said to an author who put questions to him concerning Kabbalah, the secret teachings, and the *kavvanot,* the mystical concentrations, which are directed toward superhuman effects. "You must keep in mind that the word Kabbalah is derived from *kabbel:* to accept; and the word *kavvanah* from *kavven:* to direct. For the ultimate significance of all the wisdom of the Kabbalah is to accept the yoke of the Kingdom of God, and the ultimate significance of all the art of the *kavvanot* is to direct one's heart to God. When a man says: " 'The Lord is my God,' meaning: 'He is mine and I am His,' must not his soul go forth from his body?" The moment the rabbi said this, he fell into a deep faint.

# CONCLUSION:
## WHAT KABBALAH MEANS TO ME

### "A TOOL TO HELP ME GET
### AWAY FROM THE I, I, I"

*A mystic believes that, beneath the apparent contradictions, brokenness, and discord of this everyday world lies a hidden divine unity. Just beyond the radar screens of our five senses, all being is one luminous organism. . . .*

*Consider the alternative: Can it be that reality is only what you can see and that nothing is connected to anything else? Is everything in life governed by chance, happenstance, a roll of the dice? Or, for those who believe in God's existence, is it possible that God is only involved in some things but not everything? No, for a mystic, God is not only involved in everything, God is everything. To borrow an ancient mystical metaphor: God is the ocean and we are the waves. The goal and the challenge of the mystic is to keep that awesome possibility ever present in one's consciousness.*

—LAWRENCE KUSHNER, "JEWISH MYSTICISM RECONSIDERED"

When you try to encompass a two-thousand-year-old tradition in a book as short as this one, you end up doing an awful lot of paraphrasing. You sweat over dates and subtle intellectual distinctions, you worry that you're leaving too many things out or putting in too many details. It becomes too much like homework; you start to forget that you're writing about something that lives in people's hearts—that when all is said and done, Kabbalah is an expression of feelings and faith.

All religions have their mystics, people who have somehow intuited that they are both everything and nothing, at one and the same time. That sense of organic connectedness to all things is elusive, almost impossible to sustain. Yet once experienced, it becomes the ineluctable, bedrock truth underlying all of their experience, no matter what (if any) set of religious dogmas they might believe in.

I wanted to get out and meet a real kabbalist, somebody for whom the *Sefirot* and the Four Worlds aren't just ideas, but manifestations of God—a God that's as palpable as a lover, as omnipresent as the weather. Since I live in Brooklyn, I didn't have to go very far. I could have walked up Eastern Parkway and buttonholed a Lubavitcher, or down Ocean Parkway to seek out a suitably halakhic teacher. I could have taken the subway to Manhattan and audited one of Elliot Wolfson's classes on Jewish mysticism at NYU, or refreshed myself with a bottle of cool blessings-irradiated water at the Kabbalah Centre on 48th Street. Instead, I went to Park Slope, where I met with a rabbinical candidate in the Jewish Renewal movement. An Israeli expatriate, Eyal teaches Hebrew to children and is active in the peace movement.

"What does Kabbalah mean to you?" I asked him, getting right to the point.

"It's a path," he replied, "a process. I was interested in spirituality for a long time, but it took me a while before I came to Judaism. I passed through Buddhism, Hinduism, New Age. I believed in flying saucers. When my partner of fifteen years died, that brought me back to Judaism, especially to Jewish Renewal. Before, I never committed myself to just one path, because I thought I could take a little bit from everywhere. Now I realize that when you commit yourself to a path, you deepen your knowledge and your practices.

"Religious enlightenment isn't something objective 'out there,' it isn't something separate that you can go and look at, a machine that you can make to do things for you. The Kabbalah Centre tells you, 'Just wear a red string and you'll be fine,' but that's not what it's like. For real spirituality, you need all the levels—including the intellectual part, which I had neglected for many years. The Kabbalah teaches us to keep all of the levels, all four worlds, in harmony. So for the past seven years, I've been on a path. Sometimes it's been a struggle, sometimes not, but it's always been fascinating. I found through Kabbalah what I had been looking for in other places."

"But do you think those other approaches might have eventually gotten you there too?" I asked. "To a place of real feeling, of real spiritual connection?"

He shrugged noncommittally. "Judaism enables me to go deeper, it's given me a path on which I can engage with the past teachings and learn what they mean to me. I was born in Israel, I have the Hebrew, which is a huge blessing. It turns out there was a good reason for me to be born as a Jew."

"But when you reach the end of the path—what then?" I persisted. "Won't you be occupying the same space as mystics from other faiths? Weren't you all pursuing the same goals all along?"

"Zalman Schachter-Shalomi says that when you get there—when you become transparent—it's all the same," Eyal conceded. "But the paths we take are very different. Judaism teaches that when you really study, the barriers fall through the texts. It's an intellectual path. You're drawn to it from an intellectual level, but eventually you really want to *experience* the union. Enlightenment isn't something where one day you're not and then one day you are and that's that. It's about glimpses. Mystical awareness is a time when there are no words, when thought ceases, when the constant stream of thought, the gap between one thought and the other, expands. That's the aim: to expand those moments. It doesn't have to be Jewish, and it doesn't have to be intellectual—any practice you do for a long time will help you get there."

He made an expansive gesture, taking in the plants on his windowsill, the artwork on his walls, the shelves full of books and CDs. "You can do it through the feelings, through appreciating something beautiful. You can do it through social action. When you're totally engaged in some activity where the self is not involved, where you're so focused on what you do—through art or dance or chanting—you'll get there. Music is one of the most amazing and powerful tools we have. It can even be through drugs and alcohol. Drugs can definitely do it."

"Drugs?" I say, a little taken aback.

"Definitely," Eyal declared emphatically. "That's why they're so attractive."

A molecular biologist named Dean Hamer has written a book called *The God Gene,* in which he proposes that mystical experiences are associated with the brain chemicals known as monoamines. People that we think of as being especially spiritual, Hamer says, have a genetic predisposition that causes them to process their monoamines differently than less religious people do. Drugs that shamans are known to use, like psilocybin, affect the monoamines. I find myself wondering why kabbalists, in all their thousands of years of secret, esoteric practice, never used drugs to attain a state of religious ecstasy. Or did they? Maybe that's one secret of Kabbalah that still hasn't been revealed.

Eyal interrupts my reverie. "I'm not saying that drugs are a good thing," he says seriously. "In fact they're quite dangerous. A drug might replicate a mystical experience, but it doesn't prepare you for it in any way, it doesn't teach you how to appreciate it while it's happening, how to retain its benefits when the experience ends, which it inevitably does. Since it's a drug, it will work less effectively every time you take it. The more you take it, the less powerful its effects; life will seem awful without it, frustrating with it. And then you can damage your body; you can go insane. Remember the parable of the four rabbis who entered paradise? With drugs, we tend to say 'this is not reality, it is only in the brain.' With meditation, we would never say that."

"People who don't believe in God," I say, "insist that religion is a way of sublimating the fear of mortality, that it is a denial of death. Does that play any part in your religious practice? Do you think a lot about death? Does Kabbalah console you or help you deal with it in some way?"

"I was fascinated by death and dying from a very young age," Eyal admits without hesitation. "I tried to understand what's beyond this world. For the five years that I knew that my partner Shlomo was going to die, the thought of an afterlife helped me cope. But after he died, and after we had to bury quite a few other friends who died of AIDS, death stopped being such an issue. It stopped being important to me, especially in the past four years, with the world in such terrible shape."

"Is that where *tikkun olam* comes in?" I ask.

He frowned. "A few days ago, I heard about an Israeli woman who was involved in creating cooperative artistic projects with Palestinians. She was accused of being a collaborator in terrorism and arrested; I got an e-mail asking me to contribute to a fund to help pay for her bail. The same day, Jewish Renewal sent me an e-mail to solicit a donation so they could erect a gravestone on the Mount of Olives for the Maiden of Ludmir. They asked for the exact same sum! It troubled me. Here Jewish Renewal is busy building idols while the world is falling apart around us. They should be more involved with the world.

"The focus of so much of the New Age (and sometimes I fear that Jewish Renewal is no exception to this) is *me, me, me.* For me, the whole point of Kabbalah is to get out of the I, I, I. I'm less interested in the theosophical side of Kabbalah than the ecstatic, but I study all of it. It's a discipline, a tool, a system to lead me to union.

"I was raised on a socialist kibbutz," he continues. "I was completely secular for so much of my life. But living a spiritual life doesn't mean that you don't care about injustice. For me, *tikkun olam,* fixing the world, is one of the essences of Kabbalah. For that I follow Arthur Waskow and Heschel. When you have one of these glimpses of the mystic, part of the realization you have is of the underlying unity of all things—of all people. You realize that when you do harm in the world, you do harm to yourself.

"You know," he digresses, shaking his head, "a few weeks ago, there was a big gay and lesbian march in Israel. Of course there was lots of controversy with the Orthodox. And then Israel's greatest living kabbalist, a ninety-year-old man, joined the fray. 'The gays and lesbians,' he pronounced, 'will be punished in their next lives. They'll all be reincarnated as rabbits.' And I thought to myself, is that what this is all about? Ninety years old, a tradition going back thousands of years, and this is the best it can come up with?"

It's even worse than Eyal suspected. A few years ago, this same rabbi, who is a force in right-wing Israeli politics, called upon Israelis to reinstate the biblical penalty for homosexuality: death. "Homosexuals and lesbians are not only a sickness," he declared. "They are an abomination which should be removed from every city in the country." Wire services around the world recently reported this same rabbi's offer to provide special blessings by telephone for those who are guilty of the sin of masturbation—the cause, he said, of "nearly all troubles, agonies, wars, diseases and poverty."

"I tend to be an optimist," Eyal said, shaking his head sadly. "I see the world as progressing, but in kind of up-and-down waves that eventually tend upwards. *Tikkun olam* is exactly like the *Aleinu* prayer—it's our duty to raise and praise. God made us not like the rest of the people, but with a desire to do better."

*Aleinu*

*We are duty bound to praise the Lord of all, to acclaim the greatness of the One who forms creation, who did not fashion us like other nations of the world and did not establish us as other families of people on earth, who has not defined our por-*

*tion like theirs, nor our destiny like that of their multitude. We bend the knee and bow, acknowledging the king of kings, the Holy One, blessed be He, who stretches the heavens and lays the earth's foundations, whose glorious abode is the heavens above, whose mighty Presence inhabits the loftiest heights. He is our God, there is no other. Our King is truth, there is none but Him, as it is written in His Torah: "Know this day and take it to heart that the Lord is God in the heavens above and on the earth below. There is no other."*

*Therefore we hope in You, Lord our God, soon to see the splendor of Your might, removing idolatry from the earth with false gods utterly destroyed, perfecting the world with Your sovereignty so that all mortals will invoke Your name, turning back to You all the wicked of the earth. May all who dwell on earth realize that to You every knee must bend, every tongue vow loyalty. Before You, Lord our God, shall they bend and bow, paying homage to Your glory. May they all accept the yoke of Your sovereignty and may You reign over them, soon and forever. For sovereignty is Yours, and forever shall You reign in glory, as it is written in Your Torah, "The Lord shall reign for ever and ever." And it is said, "The Lord shall be King of all the earth. On that day the Lord alone shall be worshipped and shall be invoked by His singular name."*

The *Aleinu* prayer, according to rabbinical tradition, was written by Joshua after the battle of Jericho; today it is usually attributed to the Babylonian sage Rav, who lived in the third century C.E. Originally it was a part of the Rosh Hashanah liturgy, but starting in the thirteenth century it became the closing prayer of each daily service.

Ironically, there has been considerable controversy associated with the *Aleinu*, both inside and outside of Judaism, because of its ostensible chauvinism. One line, "for they prostrate themselves before vanity and emptiness and pray to a god that saveth not," was interpreted as an explicit reference to Jesus and thus a slur on Christians. It has been removed from the Reform liturgy.

"The second part of the prayer focuses on the world as it will be," Eyal continued. "Whenever I leave services, I think how we can bring that world closer. *Tikkun olam* is like meditation—you can expand it endlessly. I know people who are addicted to it; *tikkun olam* is all they do. But there's no balance in that. The Kabbalah tells you to balance *Hesed* and *Din.*"

"But how do you reconcile your inner joy—the peace you get when you meditate—with your distress about the state of the outer world?" I asked him. "How do you balance the emotional obligations of the public and the private?"

"The public and the private can't be disconnected—they feed into each other," Eyal answers. "These glimpses of wholeness that I've been lucky enough to see, they lead me into action. Social action enables one to connect. I want to make sure that all of us share in the unity and compassion that binds us together."

A small gray cat leaps onto the chair I am seated in and places a tentative paw on the keyboard of my portable computer.

"No, Sasha," Eyal rebukes him gently. "Not now." The cat withdraws his paw and squeezes onto my lap, where he makes himself comfortable.

"I feel very down since the second intifida, since Sharon, and Bush," Eyal admits with a sigh. "But I know we can get to a better place. Economics will bring the peace; time will bring the peace. We almost had it a few years ago, we'll get there again. My optimism is a kind of messianic understanding. Things do improve. You see the cracks, but you also see that things are growing. The problem is that people are operating as opposing forces instead of trying to respect each other.

"I don't know what the future is, but I do know what I have now. What you learn through meditation is that what's really important is the present: how we live, what we do. To study, to meditate—I can't separate them. I pursue both. I don't know what God's part in it is, but I know that the one feeds the other."

# AFTERWORD:
# GATHERING THE SPARKS

## BY RODGER KAMENETZ

### WHAT I KNOW FROM KABBALAH

*Above all, kabbalah is a meditation on creation, an attempt to find adequate language to describe all that we experience.*

Kabbalah is a mystical and esoteric system. Esoteric means hidden and the Hebrew word for mysticism, *nistar,* means hidden. Not all mystical systems are esoteric, but Kabbalah is, and for a very good reason: the nature of what it hopes to describe is in its very nature hidden. I cannot explain Kabbalah sufficiently in this brief space to leave a reader knowing what Kabbalah is. I would not want the reader to think that I could do so. But I can explain what I know because of Kabbalah.

I know from Kabbalah that whatever is born—whether it is the birth of a child, the birth of the next moment, or the birth of the cosmos—emerges from a shattering and is damaged in some way. We can read the story of this imperfection in the Torah, in human history, and in our lives. It is the same pattern on different scales: a withdrawal of meaning into the mystery of itself, followed by a terrible shattering of whatever inadequate vessels we have gathered to hold meaning, followed by the effort of repair. This is the pattern in our lives over and over again—it is the thumbprint of creation pressed into every moment. I know that the first phase of creation, the initial withdrawal of meaning, gives us the freedom to make our own meaning, along with our own errors. This freedom also enables us to go back to the beginning and make a repair. In many ways our duty as human beings is to see what needs fixing, to adjust what is imperfect, and to seek to make it better. This is called *tikkun*—repairing—and it happens on many levels. On the physical level, *tikkun* is healing. On the political level, tikkun is a fight for justice, freedom, and dignity for all human beings. *Tikkun* on the spiritual level is focusing our intention with every prayer and every good deed. These levels of *tikkun* are all part of one effort.

I know from Kabbalah that God is hidden. I know that this is for a reason and is part of the mystery of creation, and of creativity. I know that the language Kabbalah uses to talk about God is necessarily obscure, not just accidentally obscure. And that understanding why it is necessarily obscure also explains why there is evil in the world, and imperfection all around. I know that our search for God involves names that are wrong, and that the process of lifting the veils is the same as the process of learning how the names are wrong, and learning the right names. We ourselves shatter and ruin the names of God by the way we use them. Only through a shattering of ourselves and the names we use for ourselves can we get a glimpse of the actuality behind the names of God.

I know from Kabbalah that all the names of God, especially the name "God," are masks and personae, are inadequate but also all we have. Our common language for talking about spiritual matters is inadequate. Language is both our gift and tragedy, and the nature of what we talk about when we talk about God is the impossibility of its being talked about. Our very efforts to talk about it obscure the subject. Yet hidden within the apparent language is a secret language which is the only proper language to suggest a being whose nature precedes time, space, and language. I know from Kabbalah that we who live in time and space dwell in the world of doubleness and duplicity. This is encoded in the first letter of the Torah, the letter Beth, which stands for the number two. And I know indeed that every letter of the Torah, if read properly, has a secret. The Torah itself is not just a book of stories or of laws—though it is also that—but it may be read with such a deep reverence for its particulars that a whole new revelation of wonder is exposed. In "The Gates of Light" by Joseph Gikatilla, for example, we see that every word in Torah is connected to a particular name of God.

I know that the reading of Torah and Bible that we have inherited from the nineteenth-century "higher criticism" is less interesting and perceptive and whole than the reading of Torah we get from a kabbalist like Gikatilla of the thirteenth century—and I feel humbled. The kabbalists saw the same seams in the text, and the same doubling and "errors" as the logical analysts who split the text into strands of J, E, P, and D—according to the God names they found used there (YHVH for J, Elohim for E, and so on)—but gave it a reading that healed the splits, and gave the work a unity and power no analyst could imagine. And I know then from Kabbalah that the soul of Torah is deeper than analytics, and that a text is not only a plaything of the mind, but can be a guardian of the soul and an opener of the heart. I know that the scholarly intellectual way of reading Torah so common today only breaks the text down into bits, and that there's a deeper way of reading: a way that performs a *tikkun* on the text, and finds the light hidden in the text. I know this from Kabbalah.

I know that the texts of Kabbalah contain the results of countless spiritual journeys, in which meditators traveled to realms and depths and came back with a new profound reading of the Torah. It contains meditations and elaborations on the book of Genesis—the secrets of creation; and on the book of Ezekiel, the secret of making those visionary journeys. People today are also meditating on creation. Some are doing it in prayers and synagogues, others in the laboratories doing stem cell research or accelerating particles in a cyclotron. And certainly we are making spiritual journeys and hoping to find an adequate language to describe what we have experienced, as the kabbalists found.

Now if people still were to ask, "All right, but what is Kabbalah?," expecting a certain kind of historical answer, let them look in the books of the great scholars, such as Gershom Scholem, Moshe Idel, and Joseph Dan. From the scholars they will know that Kabbalah is a textual mysticism, a hyper-midrash or super-commentary, using a set of symbolic relations known as the *Sefirot*. The ten *Sefirot*—ten aspects of the hidden one—provide a skeleton key for reading Torah. The Torah itself is seen as one long name of God, not a book of stories or laws at all.

The best answer to the question, "Where does Kabbalah come from?," I heard from Rabbi Zalman Schachter-Shalomi, the most creative kabbalist I've personally encountered. He told me simply and stunningly, and with a bit of mystery, "Where does Kabbalah come from? It comes from the future."

—POSTED ON BELIEFNET

# GLOSSARY

**Abulafia, Abraham.** Spanish kabbalist (1240–ca. 1291). Exponent of "Ecstatic Kabbalah."

**Adam Kadmon.** Primal man; a spiritual entity in Lurianic Kabbalah that is different from Adam ha-Rishon, the first man.

**Akiva.** Rabbi Akiva ben Joseph (50–135 C.E.). Also spelled Akiba. One of the greatest Talmudic sages and a supporter of the ill-fated bar Kokhba rebellion against Rome in 132 C.E. (he believed bar Kokhba was the Messiah). He was tortured to death by the Romans.

*Aliyah.* Literally "going up"; as *aliyah l'Eretz Yisrael,* or "making *aliyah,*" it means moving to Israel.

*Asiyah.* The lowest of the Four Worlds, the world of everyday reality.

*Atsilut.* The highest of the Four Worlds, the world of divine union.

*baal shem.* "Master of the Name," an itinerant healer and wonder-worker.

**Baal Shem Tov.** "Master of the Good Name," Rabbi Yisrael ben Eliezer (1700–1760), the founder of *Chassidut,* or Hasidism.

*Bereshit* **mysticism.** Contemplation of the mysteries of creation.

*Beriah.* The third world, where one yearns for connection with God.

*bet midrash.* A place of study.

*Binah.* The third *Sefirah:* understanding.

**Catharism.** Also known as the Albigensian heresy. Eleventh-century Gnostic movement in Provence that believed the world was created by Satan.

*Chassidut.* The Hasidic movement founded by the Baal Shem Tov in the 1700s.

**dybbuk.** An evil spirit.

*Ein Sof.* Literally, "without end." The divine essence from which the *Sefirot* emanate.

**emanations.** In Neoplatonism, hierarchically descending radiations from the Godhead that ultimately devolve into the material world.

**Four Worlds.** In addition to the ten *Sefirot,* kabbalists believe there are four worlds, or levels, of spiritual awareness. See *Asiyah, Atsilut, Beriah,* and *Yetsirah.*

*Gematria.* Methods of interpreting or encoding Hebrew, usually based on the numerical values of the Hebrew letters.

*Gevurah.* The fifth *Sefirah:* power.

*Gilgul.* The transmigration of souls.

**Gnosticism.** A belief system common in the early Christian era distinguished by the idea that the world was created and is ruled by a "demiurge," a lesser deity, and is essentially evil.

*Halakha.* Jewish law as espoused in the Torah and interpreted in the Oral Torah, the Talmud.

*Ha-Shem.* Literally, "the Name" (refers to God).

**Hasidim.** "Pious ones." Name for members of two distinct mystical movements, the *Hasidei Ashkenaz* of the Middle Ages and the *Chassidut* movement founded by the Baal Shem Tov in the eighteenth century.

*Heikhalot* **mysticism.** A variant of *Merkabah* mysticism in which adepts imagine themselves exploring the heavens and divine palaces (*heikhalot*). Common from the second through the sixth centuries C.E.

*Hesed.* The fourth *Sefirah:* love.

*Hod.* The eighth *Sefirah:* prophecy.

*Hokhmah.* The second *Sefirah:* wisdom.

**hypostasis.** In philosophy, the reification of an idea; an abstraction made concrete. In Neoplatonism, it often refers to the Godhead.

**Kalonymides family.** Leading family of the medieval German *Hasidei Ashkenaz.* Rabbi Samuel the Hasid, Jehudah the Hasid of Worms, and Eleazar of Worms were all members.

*Kan zippor.* "Bird's nest." The Messiah's dwelling in paradise.

**Karaites.** Jewish sect that arose in the ninth century c.e. in the Middle East. They accepted the Bible but rejected the Talmud.

**kashruth.** Jewish dietary laws.

*kavvanah.* Concentration in prayer, a form of meditation.

*kelipot.* (Also spelled *klippot*). In Lurianic Kabbalah, the shards of the lower *Sefirot* that shattered in the *shevirah,* the earthly husks in which divine sparks are imprisoned.

*Keter.* The highest *Sefirah:* the crown.

*Kol nidre.* Opening prayer of the Yom Kippur liturgy.

**The left.** The "left" side of the *Sefirot,* when they are diagrammed as a tree, is feminine; it is also the side of "harsh justice," where evil enters the world.

**de Leon, Moses.** Moses ben Shem Tov de Leon (1240–1305). Spanish kabbalist, probable author of the *Zohar.*

**Lilith.** Adam's first wife in some traditions; a malevolent she-demon who preys on infants.

**Luria, Rabbi Isaac** (1534–1572), called "the Ari," or lion, an acronym of his title and name. The dominant figure in postexpulsion Kabbalah.

**Maimonides, Moses** (1135–1204), the "Rambam," great Jewish philosopher, author of *Guide to the Perplexed* and the *Mishneh Torah.* His son Abraham (1186–1237) was a proponent of "Jewish Sufism."

*Malkhut.* The tenth *Sefirah:* presence. Another name for *Shekhinah.*

*Merkabah* **mysticism.** Ecstatic contemplation of Ezekiel's chariot or throne *(Merkabah);* a school of mysticism dating from the first century C.E.

**Messiah.** Eagerly anticipated king and deliverer of the Jews, whose advent will mark the end of history.

**Metatron.** An especially powerful angel. In some mystic texts he is God's subordinate on earth.

**metempsychosis.** The transmigration of souls; reincarnation.

*Midrash.* Anecdotal or allegorical texts designed to teach a moral point.

*mitzvot.* (Plural of mitzvah). A good deed, a command of God.

**Nachmanides,** Rabbi Moshe ben Nachman (1194–1270), the "Ramban." The foremost halakhist of his time.

*Ne'ilah.* Closing prayer of the Yom Kippur liturgy.

**Neoplatonism.** Third-century philosophical system that imagines the world as an emanation from God. Plotinus (204–270 C.E.), an Egyptian-born Roman philosopher, was its chief exponent.

*Netzah.* The seventh *Sefirah:* eternity.

*peah.* Also spelled *peot.* Sidelocks, which observant Jews often refrain from cutting. In Kabbalah, the beard is said to represent the moment in the unfolding of the *Sefirot* when divine grace flows through creation.

**pseudepigrapha.** Religious writings, often fictitiously ascribed to biblical characters, that are not included in the official canon. Also called Apocrypha.

**rebbe.** Generally a teacher of Torah; also used to refer to the leader of a Hasidic denomination.

**Rosh Hashanah.** The Jewish New Year.

*Sefer ha-Bahir.* "The Book of Brightness." Key kabbalistic text that first appeared in Provence in the twelfth century but is probably much older.

**Sefer Yezirah.** The "Book of Creation," a seminal text for kabbalists that probably dates to the second century C.E.

**Sefirot.** Ten emanations from God by which he manifests himself to creation.

**Shekhinah.** The tenth *Sefirah:* the immanence of God. Also known as *Malkhut.*

**Shema.** The Jewish prayer that comes closest to the *Credo.* It begins, *Sh'ma yisrael, adonai elohenu, adonai echad,* "Hear O Israel, the Lord Our God, the Lord is One."

**shevirah.** In Lurianic Kabbalah, the "breaking of the vessels" that resulted in the creation of the world.

**Shimon bar Yochai.** (135 C.E.–170 C.E.) Talmudic sage and Jewish nationalist, putative author of the *Zohar.*

**sparks.** In Lurianic Kabbalah, pieces of the divine light that are trapped in earthly matter *(kelipot);* they are reunified with God by good deeds ("raising the sparks").

**Sufism.** Muslim mysticism. Probably derived from the Arabic word *suf,* or wool, which refers to the wool cap its followers traditionally wear.

**tallith.** Prayer shawl.

**Talmud.** The vast corpus of rabbinical wisdom on Jewish law and the Torah that was assembled in Palestine and Babylonia in the centuries after the fall of the Second Temple, also known as "the Oral Torah."

**Tanakh.** An acronym for the Jewish Bible, based on *T* for Torah, *N* for *Neviim,* the Prophets, and *K* for *Ketuvin,* the sacred writings.

**tefillin.** Leather cubes containing Bible texts strapped to the arms and

head by religious Jews during morning prayers. (also called phylacteries) which is the Greek word for "amulet."

**tetragrammaton.** "Unpronounceable" four-letter name of God.

**theosophy.** Teachings about God and the world based on mystical rev-
elations.

*Tif'eret.* The sixth *Sefirah:* beauty.

*tikkun olam.* "Fixing the world." In Lurianic Kabbalah, raising sparks
by good deeds to literally repair creation; in general use it means the
commitment to social action.

**Torah.** The five books of the Bible attributed to Moses: Genesis, Exodus, Leviticus, Numbers, and Deuteronomy. It is often used to mean
the entire Hebrew Bible, as well as the Talmud and important later
commentaries.

*tzaddik.* A righteous Jew (based on the Hebrew word *tzedek,* or "justice"). Also refers to an enlightened Hasidic leader.

*tzimtzum.* In Lurianic Kabbalah, the contraction and "removal" of
God's infinite light in order to allow space for the creation of independent realities.

*Yesod.* The ninth *Sefirah:* foundation.

*Yetsirah.* The second of the four worlds, the world of worship.

**Yom Kippur.** Jewish "Day of Atonement."

**Zevi, Shabbetai** (1626–1676). A Smyrna-born rabbi who declared
himself Messiah in 1665.

*Zohar.* "The Book of Splendor." The greatest text in Kabbalah.

**Zoroastrianism.** A Persian religion founded in the sixth century B.C.E.
by the prophet Zoroaster. Its supreme god, Ahura Mazda, requires
human good deeds to assist him in his struggles against the evil
spirit Ahriman.

# NOTES

*Bible quotes throughout are from* Tanakh (Jewish Publication Society, 1985).

CHAPTER I

1  Scholem, Gershom, *Major Trends in Jewish Mysticism* (Schocken, 1974), p. 136.

6  Dan, Joseph, *The Heart and the Fountain* (Oxford, 2002), p. vii.

7  Scholem, *Major Trends*, p. 14.

13  Ibid., p. 122.

17  Green, Arthur, *Ehyeh* (Jewish Lights, 2003), p. 21.


CHAPTER 2

23  Matt, Daniel C., *The Essential Kabbalah* (HarperSanFrancisco, 1995), p. 74.

24  Scholem, *Major Trends*, p. 58.

26  Kaplan, Aryeh, *Sefer Yetzirah* (Weiser, 1997), p. 285.

28  Ibid., p. 287.

36  Dan, *Heart and the Fountain*, pp. 108–109.

37  Scholem, *Major Trends*, p. 92.

37  Ibid., pp. 103–104.

38  Dan, Joseph, *The Esoteric Theology of Ashkenazi Hasidim* (Mossad Bialik, 1968), p. 131.

38  Scholem, *Major Trends*, p. 110.

40  Kaplan, Aryeh, *The Bahir* (Weiser, 1989), p. 31.


CHAPTER 3

43  Matt, *Essential Kabbalah*, p. 121.

45  Silberman, Neil Asher, *Heavenly Powers* (Putnam, 1998), p. 77.

46  Scholem, *Major Trends*, p. 149.

47  Ibid., p. 137.

48  Trachtenberg, Joshua, *Jewish Magic and Superstition* (University of Pennsylvania, 1939), p. xi.

49  Scholem, *Major Trends*, p. 142.

50  Dan, Joseph, and Ronald C. Kiener, *The Early Kabbalah* (Paulist Press, 1986), p. 175.

52  Scholem, Gershom, *Kabbalah* (Meridian, 1974), p. 104.

53  Green, *Ehyeh*, p. 40.

54  Matt, *Essential Kabbalah*, p. 54.

63  Green, *Ehyeh*, p. 59.

65  Matt, *Essential Kabbalah*, p. 141.

66  Green, *Ehyeh*, p. 72.

68  Matt, *Essential Kabbalah*, p. 6.

70  Scholem, *Major Trends*, pp. 190–191.

72  Scholem, *Kabbalah*, p. 69.

73  Scholem, *Major Trends*, p. 254.


CHAPTER 4

78  Dan, *Heart and the Fountain*, p. 215.

81  Scholem, *Major Trends*, p. 285.

84  Scholem, *Kabbalah*, p. 261.

87  Sears, David, *The Path of the Baal Shem Tov* (Jason Aronson, 1997).

89  Buber, Martin, *Tales of the Hasidim* (Schocken, 1975), pp. 2–3.

91  Scholem, *Major Trends*, p. 329.

98  Kamenetz, Rodger, *Stalking Elijah* (HarperSanFrancisco, 1997), p. 23.

99  Green, Arthur, *Tormented Master* (Jewish Lights, 1992), p. 235.

99  Matt, *Essential Kabbalah*, p. 116.

CHAPTER 5

100  Trachtenberg, *Jewish Magic,* p. 129.

105  Excerpted in Twilight Grotto Esoteric Archives, www.esoteric archives.com.

108  Ibid., p. 89.

110  Ibid., p. 96.


CHAPTER 6

112  Matt, *Essential Kabbalah,* p. 370.

113  Matt, *Essential Kabbalah,* p. 110.

113  Matt, *Essential Kabbalah,* p. 123.

117  Green, *Ehyeh,* p. 83.

118  Cooper, David, *The Handbook of Jewish Meditation Practices* (Jewish Lights, 2000), pp. 154–156.


CHAPTER 7

122  Excerpted in Dan, *Heart and the Fountain,* p. 59.

123  Tishby, Isaiah, and David Goldstein, *The Wisdom of the Zohar* (B'nai B'rith, 1990). Excerpted in Dan, *Heart and the Fountain,* p. 139.

123  *The Zohar,* trans. Harry Sperling and Maurice Simon (Soncino Press, 1934). Excerpts available online at http://www.dhushara.com/book/torah/cardoza/zohar.htm.

129  Matt, *Essential Kabbalah,* p. 79.

130  Matt, Ibid., pp. 39–45.

138  Dan, *Heart and the Fountain,* pp. 233–236.

141  Buber, *Tales of the Hasidim,* Book 2, pp. 285, 294, 166.


CONCLUSION

144  Kushner, Lawrence, "Jewish Mysticism Reconsidered," from *The Jewish Lights Spirituality Handbook,* edited by Stuart Matlins (Jewish Lights, 2001), p. 100.

# BIBLIOGRAPHY

Aaron, David, *Seeing God: Ten Life-Changing Lessons of the Kabbalah* (New York: Berkeley, 2002)

Abraham, Azriel, and Bob Waxman, *Kabbalah Simply Stated* (New York: Paragon House, 2003)

Buber, Martin, *Tales of the Hasidim* (New York: Schocken Books, 1947)

Cooper, David A., *God Is a Verb: Kabbalah and the Practice of Mystical Judaism* (New York: Riverhead Books, 1997)

———. *The Handbook of Jewish Meditation Practices* (Woodstock, VT: Jewish Lights, 2000)

Dan, Joseph, *The Ancient Jewish Mysticism* (Tel Aviv: Israel Ministry of Defense Books, 1990)

———. *The Esoteric Theology of Ashkenazic Hasidim* (Jerusalem: Mossad Bialik, 1968)

———. *The Heart and the Fountain: An Anthology of Jewish Mystical Experiences* (New York: Oxford University Press, 2002)

Dan, Joseph, and Ronald C. Kiener, *The Early Kabbalah* (Mahwah, NJ: Paulist Press, 1986)

Fine, Lawrence, *Physician of the Soul, Healer of the Cosmos: Isaac Luria and his Kabbalistic Fellowship* (Palo Alto, CA: Stanford University Press, 2003)

———. *Safed Spirituality: Rules of Mystical Piety, The Beginning of Wisdom* (Mahwah, NJ: Paulist Press, 1985)

Firestone, Tirzah, *The Receiving: Reclaiming Jewish Women's Wisdom* (New York: Harper SanFrancisco, 2003)

Frankiel, Tamar, *The Gift of Kabbalah: Discovering the Secrets of Heaven, Renewing Your Life on Earth* (Woodstock, VT: Jewish Lights, 2003)

Freely, John, *The Lost Messiah: In Search of the Mystical Rabbi Sabbatai Sevi* (Woodstock, NY: Overlook Press, 2003)

Green, Arthur, *A Guide to the Zohar* (Palo Alto, CA: Stanford University Press, 2004)

———. *Ehyeh: A Kabbalah for Tomorrow* (Woodstock, VT: Jewish Lights, 2003)

———. *Seek My Face: A Jewish Mystical Theology* (Woodstock, VT: Jewish Lights, 2003)

———. *Tormented Master: The Life and Spiritual Quest of Rabbi Nahman of Bratslav* (Woodstock, VT: Jewish Lights, 1979)

Halevi, Z'ev ben Shimon, *The Way of the Kabbalah* (York Beach, ME: Weiser Books, 1976)

Heschel, Abraham Joshua, *God in Search of Man: A Philosophy of Judaism* (New York: Farrar, Straus and Giroux, 1997)

———. *The Sabbath* (New York: Farrar, Straus and Giroux, 1996)

Idel, Moshe, *Absorbing Perfections: Kabbalah and Interpretation* (New Haven, CT: Yale University Press, 2002)

———. *Kabbalah: New Perspectives* (New Haven, CT: Yale University Press, 1990)

———. *Messianic Mystics* (New Haven, CT: Yale University Press, 2000)

Kamenetz, Rodger, *The Jew in the Lotus: A Poet's Rediscovery of Jewish Identity in Buddhist India* (New York: HarperSanFrancisco, 1994)

———. *Stalking Elijah: Adventures with Today's Jewish Mystical Masters* (New York: HarperSanFrancisco, 1997)

Kaplan, Aryeh, *Bahir* (York Beach, ME: Weiser Books, 1989)

———. *Jewish Meditation: A Practical Guide* (New York: Schocken Books, 1995)

———. *Meditation and Kabbalah* (York Beach, ME: Weiser Books, 1989)

———. *Rabbi Nachman's Stories* (Jerusalem: Breslov Research Institute, 1985)

————. *Sefer Yetzirah: The Book of Creation in Theory and Practice* (York Beach, ME: Weiser Books, 1997)

Kook, Abraham Isaac, *Orot Ha-Kodesh* (Northvale, NJ: Jason Aronson, 1993)

Kushner, Lawrence, *The Book of Letters: A Mystical Hebrew Alphabet* (Woodstock, VT: Jewish Lights, 1990)

————. *Honey from the Rock: An Introduction to Jewish Mysticism* (Woodstock, VT: Jewish Lights, 1997)

————. *The River of Light: Jewish Mystical Awareness* (Woodstock, VT: Jewish Lights, 1981)

————. *The Way into Jewish Mystical Tradition* (Woodstock, VT: Jewish Lights, 2003)

Matlins, Stuart, ed., *The Jewish Lights Spirituality Handbook* (Woodstock, VT: Jewish Lights, 2001)

Matt, Daniel C., *The Essential Kabbalah: The Heart of Jewish Mysticism* (New York: HarperSanFrancisco, 1994)

————. *The Zohar:* Pritzker Edition, Vols. 1–2 (Palo Alto, CA: Stanford University Press, 2003)

————. *Zohar: Annotated and Explained* (Woodstock, VT: Skylight Illuminations, 2002)

Meltzer, David, *The Secret Garden: An Anthology in the Kabbalah* (Barrytown, NY: Barrytown, 1998)

Quaknin, Marc-Alain, *Mysteries of the Kabbalah* (New York: Abbeville Press, 2000)

Robinson, George, *Essential Judaism: A Complete Guide to Beliefs, Customs, and Rituals* (New York: Pocket Books, 2000)

Robinson, Ira, *Moses Cordovero's Introduction to Kabbalah: An Annotated Translation of His* Or Ne'Erav (Jersey City, NJ: KTAV, 1994)

Samuel, Judah ben, et al., *Sefer Hasidim: The Book of the Pious* (Northvale, NJ: Jason Aronson, 1990)

Schacter-Shalomi, Zalman, *Wrapped in a Holy Flame: Teachings and Tales of the Hasidic Masters* (Hoboken, NJ: Jossey-Bass, 2003)

Schacter-Shalomi, Zalman, with David Gropman, *First Steps to a New Jewish Spirit: Reb Zalman's Guide to Recapturing the Intimacy and Ecstasy in Your Relationship with God* (Woodstock, VT: Jewish Lights, 2003)

Scholem, Gershom, *Kabbalah* (New York: Meridian Books, 1978)

———. *Major Trends in Jewish Mysticism* (New York: Schocken Books, 1946)

———. *On the Kabbalah and Its Symbolism* (New York: Schocken Books, 1996)

———. *On the Mystical Shape of the Godhead: Basic Concepts in the Kabbalah* (New York: Schocken Books, 1997)

———. *Origins of the Kabbalah* (Princeton, NJ: Princeton University Press, 1962)

———. *Shabbatai Sevi: The Mystical Messiah* (Princeton, NJ: Princeton University Press, 1976)

———. *Zohar: The Book of Splendor: Basic Readings from the Kabbalah* (New York: Schocken Books, 1995)

Sears, David, *The Path of the Baal Shem Tov* (Northvale, NJ: Jason Aronson, 1997)

Shapiro, Rami, *Hasidic Tales: Annotated and Explained* (Woodstock, VT: Skylight Paths, 2003)

Sheinkin, David, *Path of the Kabbalah* (New York: Continuum, 1986)

Silberman, Neil Asher, *Heavenly Powers: Unraveling the Secret History of the Kabbalah* (New York: Putnam, 1998)

Steinsaltz, Adin, *Opening the Tanya: Discovering the Moral and Mystical Teachings of a Classic Work of Kabbalah* (Hoboken, NJ: Jossey-Bass, 2003)

———. *The Thirteen Petalled Rose: A Discourse on the Essence of Jewish Existence and Belief* (New York: Basic Books, 1985)

*Tanakh: A New Translation of the Holy Scriptures, According to the Traditional Hebrew Text* (Philadelphia: Jewish Publication Society, 1985)

Tishby, Isaiah, and David Goldstein, *The Wisdom of the Zohar: An Anthology of Texts* (Washington, DC: B'nai B'rith, 1990)

Trachtenberg, Joshua, *Jewish Magic and Superstition: A Study in Folk Religion* (Philadelphia: University of Pennsylvania Press, 1939, 2004)

Weiner, Herbert, *9½ Mystics: The Kabbalah Today* (New York: Touchstone Press, 1997)

Weinstein, Avi, *Gates of Light (Sha'are Orah): The First Translation of a*

*Classic Introduction to Jewish Mysticism by Rabbi Joseph Gikatilla* (Walnut Creek, CA: Altamira Press, 1995)

Wineman, Aryeh, *Mystical Tales from the Zohar* (Princeton, NJ: Princeton University Press, 1998)

Wolf, Laibl, *Practical Kabbalah: A Guide to Jewish Wisdom for Everyday Life* (New York: Three Rivers Press, 1999)

Wolfson, Elliot, *Through a Speculum That Shines: Vision and Imagination in Medieval Jewish Mysticism* (Princeton, NJ: Princeton University Press, 1997)

Zion, Raphael Ben, *Anthology of Jewish Mysticism* (Judaica Press, 1984).

Courtesy of the author

**ARTHUR GOLDWAG**, a freelance writer and editor for more than twenty years, has worked at the Book-of-the-Month Club, where he created Traditions, a club devoted to Jewish interests, as well as at Random House and *The New York Review of Books*.

**RABBI LAWRENCE KUSHNER** is the Emanu-El Scholar at Congregation Emanu-El in San Francisco, and has also served as visiting professor of Jewish Theology at the Graduate Theological Union in Berkeley. Prior to his move to the Bay Area, he was rabbi-in-residence at Hebrew Union College in New York City. He is the author of *Honey from the Rock: An Introduction to Jewish Mysticism*; *The Book of Letters: A Mystical Hebrew Alphabet*; and *The Way into Jewish Mystical Tradition*, a finalist for the National Jewish Book Award.

**BELIEFNET** is the leading multifaith spirituality and religion Web site. Through its newsletters and Web site, Beliefnet reaches four million people daily. It is the winner of numerous prestigious awards, including the Webby for Best Spirituality site and the Online News Association's top award for general excellence for independent Web sites. Its book *Taking Back Islam* won the Wilbur Award for Best Religion Book of 2003.